Stress Curse

Take Back Control of Your Life

Sarah P. Nooring

© **Copyright 2021 - All rights reserved.**

The content contained within this book may not be reproduced, duplicated or transmitted without direct written permission from the author or the publisher.

Under no circumstances will any blame or legal responsibility be held against the publisher, or author, for any damages, reparation, or monetary loss due to the information contained within this book, either directly or indirectly.

Legal Notice:

This book is copyright protected. It is only for personal use. You cannot amend, distribute, sell, use, quote or paraphrase any part, or the content within this book, without the consent of the author or publisher.

Disclaimer Notice:

Please note the information contained within this document is for educational and entertainment purposes only. All effort has been executed to present accurate, up to date, reliable, complete information. No warranties of any kind are declared or implied. Readers acknowledge that the author is not engaged in the rendering of legal, financial, medical or professional advice. The content within this book has been derived from various sources. Please consult a licensed professional before attempting any techniques outlined in this book.

By reading this document, the reader agrees that under no circumstances is the author responsible for any losses, direct or indirect, that are incurred as a result of the use of the information contained within this document, including, but not limited to, errors, omissions, or inaccuracies.

Table of Contents

INTRODUCTION 1

CHAPTER 1: HOW STRESS IS BEATING YOU UP 9

    DEFINING A CULPRIT 10
    PHYSICAL CONSEQUENCES 13
    EMOTIONAL AND BEHAVIORAL ISSUES 17
    A WIDER IMPACT 18
    PROLONGED STRESS DISORDERS 21

CHAPTER 2: WHAT'S STRESSING YOU OUT? 27

    A FRIGHTENING TRUTH 27
    THE MANY FACES OF STRESS 29
        Financial Stress 31
        Workplace Stress 33
        Major Life Stressors 35
        Internal Causes 37
    RECOGNIZING YOUR TRIGGERS 39

CHAPTER 3: UNHEALTHY COPING METHODS 44

    UNMASKING COPING MECHANISMS 44
    MALADAPTIVE COPING MECHANISMS 47
        Common Methods 47
        Not-So-Obvious Methods 50
        Potentially Oblivious Outlets 52
    MAKING SENSE OF YOUR CURRENT STRATEGIES 58

CHAPTER 4: HOW TO RESPOND TO STRESS 60

    EMERGENCY HELPERS 60
    BUILDING LONG-TERM RESILIENCE 64
        Change Your Mindset 66
        Apply Positive Self-Talk 67

Use Social Support 69
Adopt Acceptance 70
Learn to How Respond to Stressful People 73
Take Breaks 74
Look for Lessons 74
GETTING PROFESSIONAL HELP 75

CHAPTER 5: THE POWER OF MINDFULNESS 78

MINDFULNESS EXPLAINED 78
BREATHING EXERCISES 81
PROGRESSIVE MUSCLE RELAXATION (PMR) 84
MINDFUL DETACHMENT 86
MEDITATION 88
Letting Go 89
Mindful Decluttering 91
ADDITIONAL MINDFUL ACTIVITIES 93

CHAPTER 6: HEALTHY HABITS THAT KEEP STRESS AT BAY 99

SLEEP HYGIENE 99
BECOME ACTIVE 101
EATING RIGHT 102
GATHER THE RIGHT TROOPS 104
LAUGH OUT LOUD 105
EXPRESS GRATITUDE 106
EXPERIENCE JOYFUL ACTIVITIES 107
LEARN SELF-KINDNESS 110

CHAPTER 7: MAKING YOUR LIFE LESS STRESSFUL 115

STEP ONE: PLAN AHEAD 115
STEP TWO: GET ORGANIZED 117
STEP THREE: DECLUTTER 120
STEP FOUR: SIMPLIFY 122
STEP FIVE: PRIORITIZE 124
STEP SIX: DELEGATE AND ELIMINATE 125
STEP SEVEN: COMMUNICATE CLEARLY 126
STEP EIGHT: ASK FOR HELP 127
STEP NINE: LEARN TO SAY NO 128
STEP TEN: LIMIT YOUR EXPOSURE TO STRESSFUL PEOPLE 129

STEP ELEVEN: ELIMINATE OBVIOUS STRESSORS 130

CHAPTER 8: HARNESSING STRESS FOR YOUR BENEFIT 133

INTRODUCING EUSTRESS 133
HOW TO MASTER STRESS 138
   Leverage Stress 139
   Develop Resilience Through Positive Experiences 140
   Look for Blind Spots 141
   Adopt Self-Awareness 142
   Welcome Creativity 144
   Enhance Your Priorities 145
   Increase Opportunity 146
   Welcome Stress and Strategize 147
   Collaborate 148
   Look for Signals 148

CONCLUSION 150

REFERENCES 156

Introduction

Hans Selye once said: "It's not stress that kills us, it's our reaction to it." Stress is a common thief when it comes to your happiness, productivity, health, and everyday responsibilities, and life sure hands you a mammoth of a challenge daily. It's not uncommon to feel overwhelmed by the persistent uphill battle that seems to only become relentless and more demanding when life stands still for no one. Some days, you're not even sure how you made it through the maze of parenthood, family life, and work while you try to juggle everything at once, often dropping one responsibility here and picking up unexpected trials there.

It's madness to think that we can keep up the same routine when we wake up the next morning. Rushing the kids to get done while making breakfast and getting yourself dressed simultaneously has become the new norm. Sometimes, you don't even have time left to grab a cup of coffee before you're in the car, edging your way nearer to the front of the carpool lane, while the kids seem to have boundless energy, yelling and fighting in the backseat. You envy the dad who carries his child on his shoulders, wearing a big smile every morning. His smile is accompanied by a crisply pressed suit, and he doesn't seem to mind as the child wiggles around like a worm, pointing at everything.

What does he have that you don't? The day has just begun, and you're in bumper-to-bumper traffic, hoping that you're not late for work for the third time this week. Your boss will likely make a big deal about it, so the best you can do is daydream about the plans you have to someday start your own business and answer to no one. As you sigh, a rude driver pushes you to the curb because for some reason their time is more precious than yours. Now you're yelling, honking, and trying to find any way you can to beat the clock.

On your arrival at the office, you don't have a moment to take a breath before you're rushed into the boardroom, expected to host the presentation. It's no surprise you forgot your USB with the PowerPoint presentation at home on your desk with all the madness this morning. Somehow, you make it through half the workday, counting the minutes until you can take a break from a phone that won't stop ringing. You're finally getting that coffee, but the lunch break only fuels the stress more as you overhear a coworker talking about your company cutting out unnecessary employees, and you can't help but think you might be one of them.

Getting home is no picnic, either. Traffic is followed by homework assignments, and then it's time for dinner, which is a circus on its own. After three hours of begging your toddler to sleep, you lie on your bed, looking at your partner, and both of you feel the heavy weight of the day wash over you, carrying you into dreamland before you can even speak. However miserable, this cycle continues day in and day out. Relationships suffer, and you fear for yours, even though this problem seems to affect most people.

Your concerns lie at home, and in your career. Inevitably, you fold under the weight of this heavy burden eventually, and it took you this long to realize that stress isn't normal. Your health doesn't deserve to be this run down, and you're getting no fulfillment. You're tired of being anxious, depressed, stressed out, and sick every month. You desire to learn how to let go, and you need to relax before you snap. Sleepless nights, confusion, and brain fog aren't making life easier. You're probably not even sure why you feel overwhelmed anymore, but you know that life became more and more demanding until you couldn't cope with the fallout.

All you want is some peace. You want your relationship to thrive. You want to be a loving parent to your kids. You yearn to function normally again so that you can pursue your professional dreams to become a successful entrepreneur, but at this point, you don't have control over your attention span. You feel drained, and you've had enough. One person can only handle so much before they have to make a change. This isn't normal. How can the stress curse be a normal part of your daily life? You want to regain the power to change the direction of your future and become the best version of yourself, and it won't hurt to be happy, either.

Reaching this realization is a great stride forward. The truth is that the stress curse exists. It's in every fabric of life, and everyone suffers to some extent. According to the American Institute for Stress, the U.S. is one of the most distressed cultures in the world, with 55% of Americans experiencing stress at least once a day (Boyd, 2019). It's not only workplaces that suffer either. These are the figures for every part of the population. Moreover, a third of doctor's visits in 2018 were directly related to stress. Stress impacts everyone from parents to children, entrepreneurs to employees, families and friends.

The only way you can change your life and remove the burden is to learn how to respond to stress so it doesn't overwhelm you anymore. It is possible to fulfill your obligations while keeping your sanity, no matter who you are, and how deep you've plunged. The benefits of changing your emotional health brings a wave of opportunities, and happy days ahead. You have to start understanding what stress is, and how the many faces manifest in your life. It impacts your physical, mental, and emotional well-being, and it takes no prisoners in your relationships or productivity.

Stress is capable of affecting heart health, causing immune system malfunctions, blood pressure problems, and an emotional crutch once it transforms from an irritation to a disorder. You have to know what stresses you out the most, and you'll be surprised at what is so often overlooked. To recognize your triggers, you must look inside and out. You'll better understand the unhealthy coping mechanisms many people turn to like weeknight bar hopping, which only makes the work week more stressful.

There are less obvious ways stress can make you act out, and you'll be shocked to learn how common these responses can be. Learning to respond to stress is the only way you can move forward and leave dangerous stress management techniques in the past. There are ten tricks you can use in emergency situations, and some of them work in less than a minute! Moreover, you'll understand what you need to do so that your barriers can withstand the constant blows from life. Resilience is the key to feeling different about stress. It's the gateway to a new kind of freedom that omits the everyday pressures of life.

We examine mindfulness, how it helps you take charge of your life, and the many techniques that aren't only useful, but they're also fun. Everything is substantial and backed up by science. We delve into the science behind the brain, and how you can change the way it works when you encounter challenges. Best of all, you don't need to be a specialist to adapt to the changes or understand how they work. Some activities are as enjoyable as your favorite snack because freedom from stress requires excitement and little pleasures.

There are simple habits you need to adopt, some of which you might be eager to make time for. Overwhelmed individuals tend to believe they have no time for games, but many stress-reducing activities, which double as habits are all about fun. You'll learn the secrets behind lowering your anxiety while you take care of someone who has struggled with it for years—is that you? Changing your life is reinforced with the 11 steps to a clean and healthy schedule to ensure time doesn't run away from you. The final trick to living a happy and healthy life free from pressure is to turn the tables with a proven method so you're in charge of every response to stress.

Let's face it, stress will always be a factor, but being the master of your life isn't rocket science, either. You won't believe what you can do until you do it. My journey as a mother, sister, daughter, wife, author, athlete, and volunteer has allowed me to master the curse and every reaction I have toward stress. I was also struggling with my daily responsibilities that each role required, and the juggle between them led to a breakdown. This was the catalyst for me to reassess my life, and I sprung into five years worth of research and study to find ways I could harness the strengths that existed inside of me so I could leap ahead of my breakdown.

Mental hygiene was the main focus of my research, and I found a method that worked for me. Today, my health, happiness, and peace of mind are restored. The lessons I learned helped me manage all my responsibilities while still maintaining my self-care and sanity. I steered away from escapist coping strategies, such as alcoholism and self-medication, and I found techniques that offered relief without taking anything away from my life or health. My passion is to help others find the relief I did because I realize that stress has been accepted as the new norm of this modern world, and the truth is that it doesn't need to be. You don't need to be a prisoner of the stress curse.

If you're ready to take back control, and become the master of your future self, continue reading.

Chapter 1:

How Stress Is Beating You Up

Stress is a term everyone's familiar with to some extent. Some of us feel anxious after receiving a bad review at work, and others get a knot in their stomach before a date. Parents might feel the changes happening as their kids' voices rise quickly, and students experience stress-induced insomnia with upcoming exams. The common denominator is that we feel it. There's a reason why we *feel* stress. It's not a thought or emotion alone. It's not superficial, either. It has a physical form, and it causes physical changes. Stress impacts every part of your being, physically and mentally. Learning about what's happening inside your body is the first step to taking control of the way you respond to it. Stress can beat your body like a punching bag from inside.

Defining a Culprit

What you feel physically and mentally is a manifestation of your behavioral, physiological, and emotional response to an uncomfortable situation. You perceive a lack of equilibrium between what the situation demands and what you're capable of supplying. In many cases, stress presents a mild manifestation, in which you don't recognize physical changes. You might also not even correlate your changes to the situation until it amplifies. Take a driver approaching an intersection for example. The driver knows that crossing without yielding and distinguishing safety from danger can pose a risk to survival. The driver has a primal instinct—survival, and so do the rest of us. From the days of cavemen and primitive environments comes an instinct with which the human brain must preserve the life of its host. It's the brain's ultimate ambition to protect you from harm and discomfort. Unfortunately, your body and mind form a delicate ecosystem.

Every organ and cell work together, meaning that one fallen region causes a domino effect. The driver approaches the intersection, and without even realizing it, his brain is determining the safest reaction. He receives a quick boost of chemicals that make him alert so he's prepared for the survival demand. Often these chemicals or hormones include adrenaline, norephedrine, and cortisol. Doctor Bradley Nelson explains that this begins a chain-reaction in the entire body (Lauretta, 2020). The driver experiences heightened alertness in preparation, but the hormones released in his body can cause physical and structural changes if this release remains persistent. Let's say that the driver must cross 20 intersections today. The first intersection is normal, and his response is a quick jolt. The second intersection comes right after the first, hardly giving his body a chance to reset to its normal functions before another hormonal jolt occurs.

By the fifth intersection, the driver's responses are becoming automatic, and by the tenth intersection, he's constantly alert. He can also feel these responses in every area of his body. His mind is taking a toll, and so is his body from the muscle tension. Now, the muscles don't even release the tension because he anticipates the next intersection. Imagine how the driver feels after the twentieth intersection. His stomach muscles are in a spasm, and he's sweating, lightheaded, agitated, and his leg is cramping. Every part of his body responds to the intersections, but he's noticing it more now that he's passed through 20 of them. Nelson confirms that the driver's body becomes less and less likely to respond naturally and to reset after consistent stress.

Two major problems wreak havoc in the driver's body. His immune system is the part of his human ecosystem that repairs, prepares, and responds to trauma or injury. Usually, this happens by causing inflammation around the injured or perceivably endangered region. The hormones in his body suggest the potential for oncoming injury, so his immune system responds by protecting his body from trauma with inflammation. Putting himself in this constant state of perceived danger is allowing his body to react on auto-pilot, which can cause the body to stop the reset altogether. The same lifesaving response in his body is putting him at risk now. Inflammation is connected to various mild and severe conditions. Nelson describes the auto-immune dysfunction as the brain being incapable of recognizing that the intersections will stop at some point. Chronic stress prevails because the brain refuses to switch back to 'normal' mode, putting your immune system in an automated position, which could shut down when overworked.

Everyone experiences stress differently, so you might not feel the same sensations as the driver. It might manifest as a sudden onset of acid reflux, upset stomach, indigestion, nausea, diarrhea, or constipation. You might even suffer from an unexplained headache, and your muscles experience acute tension and aches. You may suffer from hair loss called telogen effluvium. Your response might include subtle changes like irritability and teeth grinding. Acne, excessive sleepiness, and sweaty hands are also subtler signs, some of which we tend to notice anyway. Some people experience the extreme side of manifestation with panic attacks, sleeplessness, and difficulty concentrating. A change in your appetite isn't unusual, and sudden weight fluctuations also indicate a physiological response. The immune system can even alter the efficiency of your pancreas functions and insulin or glucose levels to send your blood sugar levels into madness, bringing unexplainable and lasting fatigue.

Blood sugar levels can also cause additional problems in your body, leading to metabolic syndrome, which increases your risks for more severe health conditions. Your sugar and insulin levels also affect your moods. You might even lose your libido or sex drive. Stress has countless ways of manifesting in unique individuals, making it a valid threat to your body, so it's no wonder the immune system carries on running until it burns out. The bottom line is that stress is a perceived threat, and your body will respond, whether you control it or not.

Physical Consequences

Understanding how stress activates an immune response that keeps working is one thing, but learning about the impact this auto-function has on your physical health is another. What you feel is a loss of libido when you aren't up to romance with your partner, but a lack of sexual interest isn't the only problem. One major concern of stress is how it impacts fertility. Between the stress hormones and something called alpha-amylase, women take 29% longer to conceive, it's no surprise that stress counts for 30% of infertility problems (Levine, n.d.). Getting your stress under control is non-negotiable if you plan on starting a family. Of course, they come with their own type of stress, but being unable to have children will only make your stress and anxiety levels increase. Let's not forget about the problem infertility causes between couples, even when they think they can overcome it. However, infertility is merely one physical consequence of stress.

You must understand the more technical side of your body and brain's physiological response to know how bad chronic stress can become. A review published by Doctors Melissa Conrad Stoppler and Roxanne Dryden-Edwards puts the physical consequences into focus (Stoppler & Dryden-Edwards, 2019) based on extensive research, reviews, and longitudinal data. There are two systems actively involved in the stress response. One is called the hypothalamus-pituitary-adrenal (HPA) axis and the second is called the locus coeruleus. The HPA axis consists of the hypothalamus in the midbrain, which is responsible for sending instructions to glands in the body to release hormones and neurotransmitters. It releases a chemical called corticotropin-releasing factor (CRF), which triggers the release of a hormone in the pituitary gland called adrenocorticotropic hormone (ATCH). This hormone is released into your bloodstream and encourages the adrenal glands near your kidneys to produce the stress hormones.

Cortisol is also known as a corticosteroid, which encourages the body to reserve its resources, such as glucose, energy, fat, and carbohydrates for the stress response. Overflows of corticosteroids suppress immune function, and the HPA axis relies on a feedback mechanism to know when to stop the response. The feedback is intended to stop the production of the HTCH hormone. This is where the second system comes into play. The locus coeruleus is what sends feedback to the HPA axis, and it relies on memory and sensory input. Your senses, including smell, taste, sight, touch, and sound are sending information to the locus coeruleus, which uses memory to determine whether the threat perception has changed. This is the part of your brain that releases norephedrine, and arousal and vigilance increase. Your blood pumps faster, arteries narrow, and your heart picks up an irregular beat. Your respiration and blood pressure are being regulated by the hormone intended to wake you up so you're ready to respond to the threat.

Your digestive system and sexual or reproductive organs and desire are temporarily shut down while this happens. However, if the threat is menial or familiar, the feedback tells the brain to stop the stress response. The locus coeruleus lies within the limbic system of your brain, which is the same place memories and emotions are stored. Let's put this in simpler terms. You see a shadow, and before you know it, the HPA axis is hard at work. Adrenaline kicks in, and you're vigilant. Suddenly, the shadow moves past you, and you realize it was just a dog. The limbic system takes your memories and convinces the locus coeruleus that the threat was nothing. Now, it switches the HPA axis off. You'd think the driver wouldn't be affected by the second intersection as much if his memory reminds him that he passed safely before. Unfortunately, his limbic system is also aware of the frequent accidents at these intersections, making him unable to switch the HPA axis off. The locus coeruleus, influenced by memories, stirs fear.

One consequence of the automated dysfunction brought on by a failure to give the HPA axis feedback is neurological decline. The neurons and synapses connecting the neurons start deteriorating, especially in the limbic system. Moreover, the loss of connections and brain cells can predispose you to higher stress sensitivity and responsiveness. Once the feedback is blocked or incapable of shutting down the stress response, the immune system, which is part of the response, may start attacking cells in the body, determined to get rid of threats that don't exist. Compromised immune systems only make the struggle harder, and chronic stress doesn't make it any better. The research between sensitive stress responses and the failed immune system caused by it was linked to many severely debilitating health conditions, such as cancer, heart disease, hypertension, cholesterol, asthma, diabetes, and skin disorders. Your body can even age faster when you're living under immense pressure that doesn't allow the HPA axis to switch off.

Chronic stress wears down the immune system's original functions, making you more prone to suffer from colds and influenza. The physical distress on your body is unthinkable if you allow stress to determine the quality of your life. In this sense, stress is beating you up physically, taking away years and quality from your life.

Emotional and Behavioral Issues

Stress sneaks into every outcome in your life, including your emotional and behavioral stability. It's a unique experience for everyone. Someone might feel overwhelmed by stress, and another person might cope well, depending on their perception. Remember that stress is the discomfort felt by someone when they perceivably don't have the supply to fulfill the demand in any situation. Some people have the tools to supply the demand, but for those who don't, it can be a slippery slope. According to the Recovery Village, prolonged bouts of stress can trigger various symptoms and psychological decline (Patterson, 2019). Irritability and anger are experienced by 45% of chronically stressed individuals, fatigue and low energy are experienced by 41% of people, and the loss of interest in life and a lack of motivation are experienced by 38% of them. Anxiety and nervousness are seen in 36% of people with stress and depression in 34% of them.

Not only does prolonged stress cause emotional challenges; it also manifests as behavioral problems. Long-term and mismanaged stress is one of the main determining factors for death in the United States (US). Behavioral changes include addictive behaviors as well because these people are desperate for relaxation when their bodies and minds are struggling to calm down. Accidents are common when someone turns to alcohol or narcotics to calm emotional distress. Unfortunately, these substances only increase the likelihood of more stress, creating a cycle that beats the person up from both sides. Suicide is also not uncommon among people who suffer from debilitating stress, or at least, the inability to cope with it.

Stress demands an adjustment to changes in your environment, and it's never been easy to adjust on demand. Indeed, many people adopt tools that help them overcome this constant blow to their mental and physical health, but sometimes people just don't have the tools. Depression and anxiety become abundant issues, and the behavioral changes cause that you can't regulate your emotions, such as anger, tolerance, acceptance, and even hopelessness. The emotional instability even encourages a decline in cognitive abilities, such as concentration and memory.

A Wider Impact

There are two areas of life deeply impacted by prolonged stress. Your professional life and romantic or social life can be destroyed by stress if it's unchecked. The workplace is often seen as a source of stress, but your stress can also decrease your productivity, tardiness, and job satisfaction. A review published in the International Journal of Productivity and Performance Management sheds some light on the matter (Halkos & Bousinakis, 2010). American employers average a loss of $300 billion annually between lost workdays and stress-related healthcare.

Moreover, 80% of workplace accidents are blamed on stress-related fatigue and distraction. There are five ways in which stress impacts your productivity. Firstly, your lack of energy is a prime suspect. Indeed, adrenaline gives you a quick burst of energy, but prolonged adrenaline starts draining your stores. Secondly, a lack of focus makes it hard to pay attention to your work. Thirdly, the anxiety caused by stress makes you feel worried all the time.

Constant anxiety about what might or might not happen only takes time away from your work. Fourthly, your ability to be creative is lost when your mind wanders outside of your task. Finally, the negative effects stress has on your personality can cause you to lash out at colleagues, deteriorating your workplace relationship. Workplace relationships are important because you have to see these people each day. The most common reason why company productivity suffers is connected to five problems. The first is staff turnover because job satisfaction is at an all-time low. It's challenging to feel happy about your work when your mind constantly wanders into anxious and depressing thoughts. The second problem is an increase in tardiness. Everyone runs late once in a while, but it becomes a habit with stress. Your quality of work and colleague relationships are other major reasons why companies are losing dollars and employees. The last problem is how frequent stress-related sick days are within a company. Most visits to doctors are related to stress on some level today, and this impacts the workplace negatively.

Family life and relationships suffer under the pressure of stress, too. Seventy-five percent of extreme perceptions of stress are related to family life (Robbins, 2015). One major issue is that we all tend to carry our stress like baggage, and it follows us home from work or wherever we find it. A couple will struggle to thrive in meaningful relationships if one partner is throwing themselves into unnecessary overtime, increasing stress levels, and bringing it home. Conflicts are common between couples, and the main reasons can be a breakdown in communication, lack of support, negative atmosphere, and misguided verbal filters. Either partner feeling a lack of support feels isolated, and believe it or not, men are more likely to offer support than women. Men see their wives struggling after coming home three hours later, and might help with the dishes or put the kids to bed. Men aren't often fond of chatting about their feelings, but they offer support in other ways.

Women might even overlook their support because they want someone to talk to. They want to scream and shout because their boss upset them. A negative atmosphere builds as the couple struggles to communicate beyond their emotions. Verbal filters fall by the wayside, and often, regretful things are said. The atmosphere already changed, and words sting harder than anything. Tempers flare, and couple communication breaks down entirely. Women tend to want to offer verbal support, and men aren't always open to this. The inability of each gender to see how their partner is trying to support them is also a concern. However, a complete lack of support is common, too.

Everyone is stressed, and sometimes, we expect our partners to suck it up. What makes it worse when couples don't have the tools to cope with stress is the relationship breaks down after tensions, animosity, and resentment grow.

It's also possible for both partners to mismanage stress and take it out on each other, killing the relationship from both sides. Stress has a funny way of causing rumination, which is the brain staying focused on everything negative. An atmosphere driven by negative feelings and thoughts only breeds more negativity. Whether at work or home, your life is being affected on a wider scale if stress is unchecked.

Prolonged Stress Disorders

There are four main types of stress disorders, and they normally follow an event or series of situations where your coping mechanisms are outweighed by the demand, much like the previous driver's example. However, prolonged complications leading to these stress disorders are usually defined by more severe events. Driving through multiple intersections would only lead to these disorders if your coping mechanisms are at their lowest, which can happen after you've already developed a disorder. Remember that your sensitivity toward stress grows, making you more susceptible to having too little supply for the demand.

The first major disorder is called adjustment disorder. Every change in your life requires an adjustment period, such as divorce, career changes, the loss of a loved one, changing homes, emigrating, sudden cultural changes, and retirement. The dynamics of your life changes when you go through any of these, and even the birth of a child requires an adjustment period. The distress is typically subjective, and you might feel isolated. Feelings of emptiness, fear, loss, depression, and withdrawal are common. Your social behavior might change, and you may not be able to function at your fullest capacity for a while. Adjustment usually takes place in the first few weeks or months, and your life will return to normal. However, any adjustment period that exceeds six months is disconcerting, and it can turn into a major depressive episode.

The second condition is called acute stress disorder (ASD). ASD is an acute response that happens suddenly about a month after a traumatic event. Some people suffer subconsciously from shock and denial, and ASD happens when these barriers come crashing down. Being witness to, experiencing, or being confronted by one or numerous traumatic events can trigger this disorder. These events normally include death, the impending death of a loved one or yourself after a terminal diagnosis, an impending threat that could injure you or a loved one, and threatened physical integrity, such as the thought of losing a limb. Thirty-three percent of trauma sufferers develop ASD (Kivi, 2012). Having a history of this disorder or other mental disorders, as well as dissociative behaviors after the trauma increases your risk for developing it.

Dissociation is a symptom often missed, and it includes numbness, feeling detached, being emotionally unresponsive, and derealization, which is the inability to recognize familiar faces and environments. Depersonalization also occurs often, and it means that you can't account for your thoughts and emotions. Amnesia isn't uncommon, either, and recurring images, nightmares, thoughts, feelings, fears, flashbacks, rumination, and constantly reliving the trauma are also signs of this disorder. You might avoid people, places, conversations, or activities that remind you of the incident. Anxiety, insomnia, irritability, difficulty concentrating, restlessness, and being startled easily are also signs. The difference between post-traumatic stress disorder (PTSD) and ASD is that the latter's symptoms should resolve within three to 30 days. If not, you might have developed PTSD.

Post-traumatic stress disorder is the third major condition. PTSD is like the former condition, except that it lasts a long time unless you learn to manage it. Think of PTSD as the ASD disorder on steroids. All the symptoms from the previous disorder are present, and they only get worse with time if they remain unchecked. PTSD is a debilitating condition, and it isn't reserved for war veterans. The same conditions that cause ASD can lead to PTSD. The symptoms are divided into four categories, avoidance, intrusive thoughts, changes in the way your body physically, mentally, and emotionally responds to stress triggers, and negative changes in your mood and personality. Prolonged suffering from PTSD can alter your personality, and change the way you react to people and places.

You might have negative views of yourself and the world, and you may feel completely hopeless. You'll struggle to maintain close relationships and jobs, and you'll become emotionally numb to other people. Experiencing positive emotions becomes nearly impossible, and you'll have a lack of interest in activities you used to enjoy. Your behavior, thoughts, and emotions will become self-destructive, leading you further down the rabbit hole. Suicidal thoughts are the worst self-destructive symptom of PTSD. Seeking help and learning to manage PTSD is critical if your condition only worsens for more than a month. PTSD can lead to the final disorder if you still can't function in your daily life after a few months.

Complex trauma disorder, also known as complex PTSD, happens when you've been under prolonged and dangerous stress for months. This disorder is also commonly suffered by people who experience prolonged exposure to trauma, such as physical, emotional, and mental abuse. It develops over years of exposure and could happen if children are neglected, you've been imprisoned or tortured, or there is repeated violence and war in your close community. Emotional regulation becomes nearly impossible in this disorder, and suicidal or self-destructive behavior is more common. Problems trusting others, avoiding relationships, and repeated feelings of guilt or self-blame are also symptoms. This disorder carries many of the common PTSD symptoms, too. Learning to manage stress and seeking professional help are advised for this condition.

Now, you know what stress is and what it does to beat you up. Next, you'll learn about the reasons why stress has entered your life.

Chapter 2:

What's Stressing You Out?

You'd think it's great to believe that you're invincible. Everyone manages stress differently, and you want to be the type of person who punches stress in the face when it shows itself. There's nothing wrong with having this mindset, but no one is invincible in this world filled with stressors around every corner. The hardiest, toughest, strongest man can fold under the pressure of life, and so can you. The closest you can come to invincibility is to manage your stress response, and you can only do this if you know what it looks like. If stress was a person, the streets in every city would be even more jam-packed. It comes from both internal and external pressures. It's important to give a face to what stresses you out so that you know what to address.

A Frightening Truth

Some people believe that stress is taboo. They think it's a sign of weakness, and they're the only ones suffering from it. Stress, depression, and anxiety are all signs of flaws in our design, or that's what we think. The only truth to this fallacy is that we become afraid of sharing our burdens. We dare not speak of the taboo that is emotional discomfort. Our friends and family will surely think we're dysfunctional if we seek help. On the other hand, some people have turned stress into a daily brag. "Wow, you won't believe what I accomplished today, even while my boss was screaming at me and my car broke down in traffic." This sentence or "bragging rights" is a way some people turn stress into a normal daily experience. We tend to admire these people who survive mountains of pressure to succeed in the corporate world. Sometimes, we envy the progress they make while they brag about their daily obstacles. Indeed, some people have created a management tool belt for stress, but in many cases, this person is waiting for the one stressor that pushes them over the edge.

Just because they overcome multiple stressors daily doesn't mean they won't break, especially if they're misinformed about the best ways to handle it. Avoidance or ignorance doesn't make anyone invincible. Facing your stress head-on, and determining how you respond to it can make a huge difference, but it can't protect you from the accumulation of negative stress if your guard is down. You'll learn more about the successful people who use stress to their advantage later, but they aren't immune. They know how to distinguish between stress that enhances or declines their lives. According to the American Institute of Stress and the Global Organization for Stress, there isn't a person who is immune to the effects of change

(Patterson, 2019). Regardless of your gender, ethnicity, culture, lifestyle, age, and even religion, you are no more immune to it than anyone else. The statistics show the frightening truth behind stress. Thirty-three percent of people report suffering from extreme stress, 77% of people report physical health changes due to stress, and 73% of people report mental health changes from stress.

Forty-eight percent of people find it difficult to sleep because of stress, 75% of Americans succumbed to moderate to high stress in the last month, and 80% of Americans suffer from workplace stress. People might look immune to the effects of stress, but they don't deny its burden in their lives when they aren't confronted by friends or family. They don't try to hide it, and acknowledging stress can help them take the first steps toward proper management. Before moving ahead, what are your stress levels right now? Do you fall into the statistics? If not, ask yourself the same question until you answer it honestly. You're not reading this book for giggles. If you answer yes, it's time to identify the stress in your life by putting a face to an idea.

The Many Faces of Stress

Defining your stress doesn't happen overnight because it has so many faces. Some examples of stress include routine pressures in the home, at work, in school, and your daily responsibilities, which are the accomplishments you need to achieve. Daily responsibilities aren't always about promotions or parenthood. Sometimes, it's about being responsible to yourself for your health. You're responsible for eating healthy so that you don't suffer from the same disorder that runs in the family, which might be diabetes. In many cases, stress is caused by tasks, experiences, and changes you need to make to either keep your life running smoothly or to improve it. Other common examples include sudden negative changes, such as divorce, unemployment, illness, or an abrupt end to a friendship. Perhaps, your employer isn't satisfied with your performance, and this naturally makes you feel stressed. Traumatic changes in your environment or community also ignite stress. Perhaps, you were involved in an accident that changed the dynamics of your daily life.

You might be traumatized by a natural disaster or pandemic, such as the coronavirus \(COVID-19). War, assault, and any injuries to yourself or others are also traumatic. They begin a state of change where your direct environment is influenced. However, most people can overcome trauma naturally with time, but you've learned about the four major disorder concerns that can develop if you don't have the capacity to manage them. These events and experiences are external factors, but you also have internal factors promoting unhealthy stress management. The way you think and respond to stress can determine how you handle the most common external causes. Money, work, family, personal health problems, the ill-health of loved ones, the economy, job stability, personal safety, and housing costs are among the most common types of external stressors. The future of the nation, violence, or crime in your community, and the political climate can change your perspective because of fear and anxiety brewing in the background. Let's break the main stressors into categories so that you can pinpoint the culprits.

Financial Stress

Money might not make the world go round, but it does make your life more manageable because no one can live, work, or thrive without the necessities. According to a survey by Northwestern Mutual, 44% of Americans consider money to be their dominant source of stress (Hill, 2018). Only 25% of them marked poor relationships as their main stressors. Two of the main culprits of financial stress are credit card debt and student loans. Credit card debt smashed a record of $1 trillion by the end of 2018, and student loans jumped more than 150% over the preceding decade. Sadly, 25% of Americans have no savings. A bad financial situation only leads to poor health circumstances. The most common symptoms suffered by people under financial stress are depression, anxiety, digestive issues, migraines, insomnia, hypertension, and heart attacks.

Financial stress is of the unrelenting kind because it is a natural response to not having enough resources to meet the demand of a situation. So, it's no wonder money plays such a huge role in it. College students make loans to meet the demand of studies, but they're left with immense debt after they graduate, placing them in a predicament for many years in some cases. As long as the debt looms over them, their supply will always struggle to meet the demand. Anyone who has no savings also struggles, especially in challenging times like this. Economic health has declined due to the pandemic, and this means that the demand is increasing, but it impacts people without savings more than anyone else. Consider how many people had to start working remotely. Others simply lost their jobs after months of lockdown and other restrictions. Wages were either decreased or they became non-existent. Without savings, many individuals and families have experienced a landslide downgrade. It's impossible not to stress under these circumstances.

The financial conundrum was happening long before the pandemic though. Credit card debt has always been a problem. The interest rates alone are a crime. People start sitting in financial-bubbles due to the heavy weight of debt, and there just isn't money to meet the demands anymore. This can even snowball into other problems. People stop taking care of their health because it costs too much money. They start eating poorly because it costs less, and this only increases their stress levels. Lower incomes lead to higher stress. It doesn't matter how much stress your workplace brings when you become desperate to meet the demand. Being employed is better than being incapable of buying food, paying debts, and affording healthcare. You might take a job that places you in an environment conducive to stress enhancement. The worst part of this cycle lower-income families are prone to experience is that they often don't have the financial resources to cope with or manage their stress. They might even turn to unhealthy management methods, increasing their likelihood of additional stress.

Financially-strapped individuals have the added stress of minimal support, and they might not even have transport to reach it. Understanding how financial stress impacts our lives can also be intertwined with cultural differences. Growing up in a low-income community puts you at a cultural disadvantage, even before you're old enough to create your own supply for the demand. For this reason, ethnicity can predispose you to higher stress susceptibility if you have fewer resources at your disposal, such as money.

Workplace Stress

Workplace stress often tops the main causes because it's where we spend most of our days. It's not only a time-factor, but it's also about the control our work places over our lives. Without work, there are no finances or stability, which pushes you right back to financial stress. Your job defines much of who you are and what your life becomes. Having the right job can increase your overall life satisfaction because it provides a purpose, which happens to bring money or resources for the demands of life. However, workplace stress comes in many forms, and the fact that you spend most of your waking hours at work doesn't make it any easier if you identify with any of the common workplace stressors. The first one happens to be your happiness in the workplace. Being unhappy with your job only makes it a daily uphill battle. You might have too much responsibility or a heavy workload.

Every person has a capacity, and overwhelming yourself in a key area of your life leads to stress. Working long hours or too much overtime also breaks your capacity because everyone needs a balance between work and home life. Poor management can also increase your stress, especially when your expectations are unclear. How must you thrive at work if you don't know what to do? Not having a say in the decision-making processes also defeats your happiness. Working in a dangerous environment only adds to the list of stressors. Perhaps, you're a police officer, being exposed to crime and violence daily. This takes its toll, even when you think you're managing fine. That's why many officers seek counseling. Other dangerous jobs might include toxic environments, which can have more than one connotation. Firstly, your colleagues and employer might be toxic people, always belittling your hard work. Secondly, your environment could be toxic with chemicals and harmful substances that cause poor health. Job insecurity is another common stressor in the workplace. The risk of being terminated is not something you want looming over your head, and you also don't want to miss out on a promotion.

Sometimes, workplace stress is as simple as having a shoe on the wrong foot. Giving speeches in front of colleagues is a difficult task if you're afraid of public speaking. Some jobs require certain responsibilities, but putting yourself in a job that makes you uncomfortable is an environment that breeds anxiety. Workplace discrimination and harassment are also concerning, even though there are many new policies to prevent this. A construction company can't always keep an eye on how their employees treat the worker on site who is foreign. Depending on the employer, they might or might not believe the worker if they decide to speak up about discrimination. Finally, the loss of a job or even retirement can be stressful. You've been with the same company for 40 years. Retirement is the goal, but it's a major life change that starts impacting you even before you retire. The fears about the future are real. Have you saved enough to retire comfortably? Will the economy remain stable enough to ensure this?

Major Life Stressors

According to the American Psychological Association, the list of stressors in descending order of priority in America is work pressure, money problems, health, relationships, poor nutrition, media overload, and sleep deprivation (Batson, 2011). Moreover, they also warn that stress is a major health problem in America. Stress isn't only taking away from people's health. It's also taking their productivity, happiness, and meaningful relationships. Stress bashes your personal and professional life. Major life events and changes are other sources of larger stressors, which come at their whim, and you're not always likely to predict them. Major life events include the loss of a loved one, divorce, and even getting married. Indeed, you'd expect the loss of a loved one to deter your immunity to stress, but getting married also requires changes. In most cases, it's a change of home or family dynamics when two people commit. Moving home can also be stressful because it removes you from what your mind became familiar and comfortable with.

Getting married might even require you to adopt children that aren't yours, and suddenly, everything in the home must be shared. Your family responsibilities grow, and so do your stress levels. Getting divorced is the opposite, but it still requires a complete change in environment and family dynamics. Losing a loved one is painful, and you can't predict the death of your family, but you know that it requires adjustment to a new life without them. This can be devastating because your hopes, plans, and dreams change when the person's gone. However, beyond these three major life changes lie another collection of stressors.

A new job or a new lifestyle can also cause stress. Lifestyles are how we face each day, but sometimes, we need to make changes, such as losing weight to avoid health problems. Even planned life changes are stressful. Becoming a parent automatically duplicates your responsibilities, particularly time and money. Of course, it's a wonderful day when you become a parent, but never underestimate the stress it can bring.

Unexpected or sudden life changes are also concerning because it's easier to prepare your stress management for expected changes. Theft, natural disasters, assault, and violence aren't expected. Losing your home and everything you worked for in a hurricane will be followed by months or years of adjustment. Losing your dignity and personal safety when someone grabs your purse and runs is another major life change because it impacts your mind for some time. Abuse and physical assault change the way you view yourself and others, and it can prevent you from coping with previously-menial stressors.

Awkward social situations are also common life stressors. Your social dynamics impact your life daily, even if you weren't harmed in any way. The fear of public speaking, meeting new people, or chatting to a romantic interest can cause stress if not managed right. Other major life stressors are when someone becomes ill. You might need to help care for them, adding to your potentially overflowing bucket of responsibilities. Whether you're diagnosed with a chronic illness or it happens to someone you care about, you'll be suffering from the emotional fallout.

Internal Causes

The amount of fear you experience during any external stressor depends on your internal coping mechanisms, which comprise a few factors. Underlying fears are an obvious reason for being overwhelmed. The fear of flying stresses you out during travel, and the thought of failure makes your self-expectations at work cause a lot of stress. Stress also has a lot to do with your perception of the situation. You might perceive the demand being greater than your resources if you've had a poor experience with the same situation before. Your self-esteem, locus of control, thought processes, and beliefs can change your perception. Feeling uncertain or being unable to control the situation turns a mole's hill into a mountain, and your perception changes depending on your predisposition to think positively or negatively. Your beliefs encumber your opinions and expectations, which are normally set unrealistically by society.

You expect to be promoted at work because you've worked hard. However, your perception starts changing about the probability when it doesn't happen in your expected time. A lack of emotional resilience or flexibility is also an internal cause of stress. Being able to adapt to the situation requires you to have coping mechanisms. Resilience doesn't make the problem disappear, it only makes you more capable of managing it, which is something you'll adopt in the coming chapters. Resilience also depends on the experience you have with the stressor you face. Two more internal factors cause stress. Everyone is capable of managing so much at once, and exceeding this limit leads to overwhelming consequences. Secondly, the amount of support you have while facing the situation also determines your outcome. A lack of support stresses you more.

Recognizing Your Triggers

Every cause of stress is called a trigger. Identifying these triggers is the only way you can eliminate what needs to go and learn to manage what can't be changed. Knowing your triggers already allows you to respond differently. Start your recognition by choosing which categories your main stressors fall into from the list below. You might fall into numerous categories. Recategorizing each stressor also helps, so give each one an 'e' for eliminate, 'r' for reduce, and 'c' for cope with. The 'e' markers will be eliminated from your daily life, which happens over time. For example, you can eliminate stressors that you have some control over, such as breaking ties with a friend who only brings you down. She's always talking about the negative side of life, and she makes you feel anxious. The 'r' markers can be allocated to stressors you can't really remove, but you can reduce your exposure to them. Let's say that your chosen mode of transport to work has increased your stress levels. You can reduce this, but you can't eliminate it because you still need to work.

You can rather replace your subway rides with a carpool three times weekly until you can afford your own car. The 'c' markers are stressors you can do nothing about. You can't change your medical diagnoses if you have cancer, but you can learn how to cope with it. The list of categories is as follows.

Category one is "family stress," which includes relationships, financial problems, and children.

Category two is "emotional stress," which includes individual fears or internal factors.

Category three is "change stress," which includes any life change that makes you uncomfortable.

Category four is "social stress," which includes social awkwardness, friendly relationships, and social expectations.

Category five is "work stress," which includes performance fears, insecurities, toxic workplace environments, and job dissatisfaction.

Category six is "decision stress," which includes procrastination and the failure to decide what's best for you.

Category seven is "physical stress," which includes sleep deprivation, poor health, bad nutrition, and disability.

Category eight is "environmental stress," which includes toxic air, community problems, and a lack of personal space.

You could add as many stressors under each category as you feel necessary, but you need to determine the possibility of eliminating, reducing, or coping with each one as well. Take a moment to assess your day-to-day life, and see which triggers are the most prevalent. Effective management only happens once you identify your triggers so that you can develop the strategies that work best for your unique life. Elimination and reduction also help you to experience fewer stressors, leaving your internal causes of stress better off. Gaining an awareness of what triggers your stress also allows you to intercept the factors during the early-onset of stress so that your day won't be overwhelmed by a vast ocean of stress at once. Sometimes, it can be tricky to find the precise causes of your stress when life seems so overwhelming. Then, it helps to narrow the potential causes down by focusing on your stress response as it happens. The next time you feel stressed, pay attention to your response and how your mind and body behave.

The first place you must pay attention to is your breathing. Notice whether your breathing changes when you're faced with a potential threat. Does it become shallower and faster? What's happening in your body while you feel anxious? Perhaps, your palms become sweaty or you can feel your heart racing a bit. Close your eyes and recognize these physical changes during stressful situations. You might feel a temperature change, and your muscles might tense. Notice where your muscles tense, and focus on this region as it changes. While recognizing the physical changes, pay attention to your mind, too. If you could describe in one or two words how you feel at this moment, what would that be? Describe your mood change so that you become aware of it.

Learning to understand how your body and mind change during stressful situations helps you identify the triggers that cause it. Now, you know what triggers your stress response, but you need to learn what to avoid before adopting your toolbelt of coping mechanisms.

Chapter 3:

Unhealthy Coping Methods

What is your first instinct when you feel stressed out? What is the first idea or response that brings you comfort? Perhaps, you prefer to avoid the issue. You might be the bar-hopper who copes with their stress by drinking copious amounts of alcohol. Unhealthy coping mechanisms are often used in an effort to manage stress, but these habits can be counterproductive to your health and well-being in the long run. Moreover, these coping tools we adopt over time exacerbate the problems we face, turning a menial stressor into something unfathomable. It's time to determine what you use when you feel stressed so that you can realize how harmful it is.

Unmasking Coping Mechanisms

Everyone tells you to cope with your stress, but do they explain what the different types of coping strategies are, and what they lead to? A coping mechanism is a habit you gain over time. It doesn't spring up overnight. Unfortunately, habits can be good or bad, and so can your responses to stress. Negative habits don't erase the problem. They only make it worse. They might even lead to numerous other problems in your home, work, relationships, and health. Quite frankly, coping mechanisms offer a crutch to avoid the painful fallout of the stressor by offering a distraction. The main reason why we keep using these negative strategies is that they often offer instant relief. However, the problem doesn't just vanish. Remember that every stressor is a face. Now, imagine the driver in chapter one sees each traffic light as a face. What would happen if the driver simply places a mask over this face each time? Is he better off, or is he in greater danger? Not only is he pretending that the stressors aren't there. He's also putting himself in greater danger by approaching traffic lights while he can't see if it's his turn to go or not.

The mask we place over stressors with unhealthy coping mechanisms blinds us from the stress momentarily, but the driver might push through a red light. His emotions and thoughts surrounding the stressor are masked, but we can't always hide away from fear. It won't go anywhere if we do. This is where the difference between adaptive and maladaptive coping mechanisms come into play. Throwing masks over the traffic lights is a maladaptive strategy. Facing the traffic lights and using a simple breathing technique upon your approach is an adaptive mechanism because you can still comprehend the real threat posed by the stressor. The same applies to any area of your life. You walk into your employer's office, and they request you stay and work overtime for the third night in a row. A maladaptive strategy might be to lash out, which costs you your job and reputation. An adaptive response would be to count to 10, take a deep breath, and calmly explain your reasoning. Which response do you think will work better?

A maladaptive response to stress or a negative coping mechanism is anything that exacerbates the unwanted outcome. It offers no solution to the original problem. Addictions are known as maladaptive habits, and coping mechanisms can also be an addiction. You'll always prefer your method of managing a situation because you have experience with it. Trying something new is scary enough. Gambling, narcotics, alcohol, and binge-eating are common maladaptive habits, but the lesser-known addictions can include exercise, avoidance, or Netflix binges. You must learn how to cope with the stressors you have no control over, but it must be part of a balanced stress management strategy. An addiction is anything you're obsessed with, repeatedly do, even though it brings no benefits, or it uses your time and attention so that you can't lead a full life.

Even your thought patterns can become addictive, which is common in cognitive distortions. The bottom line is that you'll adopt coping mechanisms, but the outcomes must offer a solution, even if it's just to calm down before responding to the stressor with a rational mind. There must never be a negative outcome.

Maladaptive Coping Mechanisms

Alcoholism isn't the only negative coping mechanism. Some are obvious, and others aren't. Some maladaptive responses to stress are behavioral, and others are mental, changing the landscape of how your mind works with time. Irrespective, your strategies often lie somewhere between both. Our thoughts and emotions trigger behaviors, so the two aren't exclusive from each other. Let's take a look at the most common coping mechanisms and those that aren't as obvious.

Common Methods

A few methods are quite obvious because we want to drown our painful emotions and fears in a glass of bourbon or wine. The first obvious method is when we consume excessive amounts of alcohol, or we partake in chasing the magic dragon. Alcohol dependence is probably the most common negative strategy because being inebriated allows us to numb the feelings we experience. Getting drunk happens in minutes for most people if they're using alcohol to numb themselves, so it provides immediate relief, which seems like a good idea at first. Alcohol dampens your stress response by feeding it with the same hormones intended to switch it off, such as dopamine (Liquido, 2014). Dopamine is also part of the reward system, which is activated by any addictive behavior.

Simply, alcohol dampens the emotional outcry, but it has lasting effects if consumed in excessive amounts. Alcoholism is connected to addictive behaviors, which can even direct you to worse substances, long-term health defects, such as liver failure, and it can also kill you. It's not only alcohol poisoning that could take your life. It's also the inhibitions you lose along the way to the "drunk-hood." Your stress response is supposed to protect you from genuine dangers, and your response time is limited or non-existent when you're driving under the influence. Alcohol is also a depressant, and that's why it inhibits emotions, but you always wake up feeling worse with a hangover. Having a single drink at the end of a long day is acceptable, but excessive drinking is dangerous.

Cigarettes or nicotine are another stimulant that suppresses the stress response, and any smoker will tell you that they smoke to cope with stress. Smoking has been related to lung cancer, heart disease, and stroke. It increases your alertness, putting your body into a heightened state of responsiveness, but the average smoker might light one up every hour. This means that you're putting yourself into a stressed mode every hour, or at least, your body and mind are reaching it. The HPA axis perceives cigarette smoke as a dangerous substance, which is true, so that's why your heart beats faster after a cigarette. You're stimulating your body. You might feel good at the moment, but you're damaging your body, so nicotine isn't a healthy coping mechanism, either. Stimulants can increase your stress levels and cause anxiety.

Stress eating is another obvious mechanism. Even the name says it all. It's also more common than you think. Twenty-five percent of Americans under or overeat when they feel stressed (Liquido, 2014). It goes either way, depending on the person. Some people crave sugar and carbs while others lose their appetites instead. Sugar gives you a quick mood elevation, but your glucose levels tend to crash after two hours. Both stress eating strategies come with negative side-effects. Eating too little can cause fatigue, weakness, mood swings, and an inability to focus. Eating too much leads to weight gain, chronic fatigue, or malnutrition from the body being unable to absorb and store vital nutrients. Weight gain is only another cause of stress, so this coping mechanism exacerbates your stress as soon as you bite into that slice of cake. Junk food, which is what we tend to turn to in times of stress, is the worst decision we can make. Poor nutrition only causes hormonal imbalances, making it harder to manage stress.

Self-harm behaviors are also a way for some people to cope with stress. Believe it or not, some people think that cutting or harming themselves takes away stress. Keep in mind that this isn't suicidal. Suicidal people are in distress and need immediate assistance. However, we're talking about self-harm addicts who tend to cut themselves. This behavior offers a temporary and immediate distraction from the emotional pain, but the consequences of their actions will always outweigh their ability to cope. For example, the scars won't vanish overnight, even if the person gets a call from a potential employer tomorrow morning. They'll have to cover the scars, and this alone causes more stress. Please note, anyone with self-harm tendencies should seek professional help. It's not okay that you can't cope with your stress. This book will give you many tools to supplement your therapy, but please seek help.

These make up the obvious choices we turn to in times of stress, but there are more coming.

Not-So-Obvious Methods

Don't be mistaken, these methods are also common, but they're not as obvious. The first culprit has to be coffee because many people use it as a stress-reliever. Little do they know that coffee, or the caffeine in it, causes more stress. Any stimulant provides an initial burst of adrenaline, which makes it a common strategy to overcome perceived threats. Let's say that you're rushing to finish a project at work. You turn to coffee to get you through the pressure, but it can make matters worse. There's nothing wrong with a cup of coffee now and then, but people who use stimulants like coffee, energy drinks, and caffeinated sodas are consuming lasting effects. Your body becomes unable to absorb adenosine, which is the chemical required to calm it down, and this can last up to six hours (Liquido, 2014). You get an initial boost of adrenaline, which inhibits adenosine, and it's followed by dopamine to make it another addictive substance. Now, you understand why you can't sleep at night if you're pumped on caffeine.

Sleep deprivation won't help you complete the project or put your best efforts into it.

Sleep is another less obvious coping mechanism for stress. Sleeping too much is a common method used by people who want to avoid stress, but sleeping too little is another strategy, which doesn't seem as obvious. Surely, you want to sleep to calm your mind down, but some people use the excuse that they need to calm their minds before sleeping, and this is often done by adding the binge-worthy Netflix to their nightly schedule. Sleeping too much places you at risk for obesity, which can lead to diabetes, but sleeping too little also has its disadvantages. A healthy sleep schedule has immense benefits for your health, but sleep deprivation only aggravates anxiety and can even impact your memory. The human brain cycles through multiple stages of sleep during the night, and the rapid-eye-movement (REM) stage is where memories are being stored. That's why you often dream during this stage. The REM stage comes after the lighter stages, so you need to sleep long enough to cycle through them throughout the night.

Self-medication is another less-obvious sign of unhealthy coping strategies. Muscle relaxants, pain medications, and numerous over-the-counter (OTC) drugs are consumed to fall asleep when people feel stressed. They even take OTC sleeping pills because they can't sleep. Admittedly, some people take medication because they feel unwell during stressful times, but not knowing why your body pains isn't going to provide a solution. Stress causes pain and other symptoms, and it helps to know why you're feeling the way you do. Imagine taking a cotton ball and trying to plug a hole in a dam with the water already breaking through. These medications are the cotton balls, your stress levels or health conditions are the gushing waters, so there's no way the cotton balls can solve a problem if the problem is being covered with balls that can't permanently stop the waters.

Lashing out at friends and family is another less obvious coping mechanism, only because they don't know why you're moody in most cases. Indeed, you might feel better once you get your stress and negative emotions off your chest, but what are the consequences? Moments later, you're feeling guilty, which only causes more stress. You don't raise your self-esteem by stepping on other people, even strangers. You end relationships by taking your emotions out on other people, and this chips away at your social crowd, stressing you out more because you lose your support network. You can't manage your stress healthily if there's no one to support you.

This brings you to the next set of coping mechanisms you need to watch out for—the oblivious outlets.

Potentially Oblivious Outlets

There are ways we cope with our stress that fly under our radars. Some of us are aware of these coping mechanisms if someone points them out, but they're commonly hidden under the guise of what we believe is acceptable in stress management. Some methods seem harmless, but they're our dirty little stress tools, even if we don't recognize them. Everyone throws themselves into a different scenario when they feel stressed.

The first oblivious outlet is to overwork yourself. Indeed, working provides a distraction from everything going wrong. Throwing yourself into a project allows your mind to stop ruminating on the negative feelings. The main problem is that your subconscious mind doesn't switch off as easily as you think. It keeps focusing on the fears simmering under your distraction. The second problem is that you're prone to make mistakes when your mind isn't focused enough on your work. Realizing your mistakes will increase your stress levels, and fixing them becomes another challenge.

Social withdrawal might seem like an obvious coping mechanism, but it isn't. You're faced with a challenge in your day, so you choose to isolate yourself in bed for days to recover from the setback. Admittedly, crawling into bed seems like a dream, but avoiding your friends and family only means that you're removing your social support. Prolonged social withdrawal is also a common sign of depression, which makes it harder to cope healthily with your stress.

Compulsive spending is another oblivious coping mechanism. Even though it's tempting to splurge a little because it makes you feel better, you need to know why it does this. Financial stress is one of the major causes of adjustment challenges, and spending money you haven't budgeted for leads to financial instability, but it's more than this. You'll succumb to feelings of shame and guilt when you allow compulsive spending to rule the roost. Moreover, compulsive shopping is an addiction. Shopping under the impulse to ease the burden of stress releases dopamine, serotonin, and epinephrine, which are the same feel-good hormones experienced during narcotic or alcohol abuse (Shifts, 2019). Retail therapy is often missed and underestimated as a maladaptive coping mechanism, but it's a dangerous one.

Wallowing, pitying, and dwelling on your stress is another oblivious strategy. Admittedly, it's all we can manage to do in times of great tribulation, but it keeps the mind latched onto ruminating thoughts, which stir negative emotions. You won't move any closer to genuine stress relief when you dwell on the problem. Self-compassion and strategic planning are better suited to finding a solution, but pitying yourself is like licking your wounds with a tongue made of swords. It will damage the wound further. Stress and feelings of helplessness will increase, which defeats the purpose of using this as a coping mechanism.

Another strategy you must be aware of is avoidance coping. Avoiding your stress prevents you from dealing with it. Avoidance coping isn't just about running away from the stressor. It also includes habits like rumination, procrastination, and passive-aggressive behavior. You're only hurting yourself more by ruminating on the negative side of a problem. It doesn't give your mind the freedom to embrace potential solutions. Procrastination also becomes a crutch because the problem won't go away just because you delay your interaction with it. Passive-aggressiveness is when you make excuses to avoid the problem. These are three major avoidance coping behaviors. You change your behavior to avoid thinking about it, feeling fear, and doing something complicated, even if it could solve the problem.

Avoidance is a maladaptive coping mechanism because it doesn't bring you any closer to a solution. To overcome stress, or to manage it successfully, you need to deal with it. Avoidance coping comes in two types. The first type is the inactive one that allows you to ruminate and grow further away from the solution. The second type is active avoidance coping, which is a healthier option if you strategically use it to take a quick walk through the park to clear your mind before tackling the problem. However, inactive avoidance can cause serious problems in your life. Relationships can't thrive if you avoid conflict, even if the disagreement is menial. Communication is the key to success between two people, whether they're friends, family, or spouses. Avoiding conflict won't bring you closer because you aren't talking about the problem and finding a mutual solution.

You're ignoring it, pretending that it doesn't exist, and becoming defensive. This could end a relationship because your friend feels disrespected, unloved, and undermined. Once again, avoidance becomes a precursor to losing your social support network. Another common consequence is when you believe that your problems will shrink if you avoid them until your mind is more capable of managing them, which is especially true for anxious people. You're anxious about your presentation in front of 100 colleagues this afternoon, so you ruminate on the fear, allowing it to grow. Even worse, your preparation time shrinks, adding additional stress when you don't have enough time to prepare. Imagine you're looking at an abstract image. You can't make heads or tails from it, but you keep focusing on it until you see an image.

What looked like a tree at first now became a horse's head. You can't unsee it once your mind makes sense of it. What do you think happens when you focus intently on your fears, giving them time to form a clearer image in your mind? You'll struggle to see past them if you give them enough power. This is how you turn anxiety into greater anxiety when you ruminate on it. You place it under a microscope, and the tree that once was a vision that carried a few potential relaxation ideas becomes a distant memory. It's never easy to face your stress, but avoiding it comes with potential risks that could exacerbate the feelings. Losing your support network is detrimental to your future ability to cope with stress. You'll enter a cycle of avoidance that snowballs into greater stress and anxiety.

The more you avoid fear, the more you'll fear the same situations, so what would be a simple disagreement between two people becomes a huge burden next time. Avoiding your fear of public speaking won't make it easier, either. It only gives your mind a reason to fear it again. Your confidence dwindles after a few avoidance experiences, making you more vulnerable to the cause of your stress. Coping mechanisms should be active, which includes two types. Active-behavioral coping is when you change your behavior toward the stressor so that you can resolve it, and active-cognitive coping is when you change your thinking so that you don't become overwhelmed by the stressor.

Finally, negativity is another automatic response to stress that also doubles as a coping mechanism, but it only tears your barriers down. This strategy is often ingrained in your mental processing, making you pay attention to the threats over and above the potential solutions. It's common for anyone who suffers from chronic stress or the stress disorders mentioned in chapter one to suffer from negativity. Their HPA axis is conditioned to perceive threats as constant and dangerous. Their minds will automatically look for the worst in every situation, making sure it's ready for any type of response. This has to be the least obvious coping mechanism because it isn't something we choose to do.

Rumination and procrastination are chosen responses to stress, but negativity sneaks up on us, changing our thought patterns and creating a cycle where we dwell on the negative feelings and thoughts. Having this as your default coping mechanism is difficult to recognize. The best way for you to identify it is to pay attention to your first responses when you're faced with discomfort. Does your mind wander off to the darker side? Do you magnify the problem or expect the worst? Why do you do this? The last question is the most important one. Sometimes, we seek a primal level of support, wanting our friends and family to accept the levels of stress we face, so we magnify the issue so that they agree with us. This oblivious coping mechanism isn't only about your thoughts and emotions turning negative. It's also about your pursuit of validation from your support network. Consider whether you seek this validation by magnifying the stressor.

This concludes the main unhealthy coping mechanisms you might use. Keep in mind that you might use multiple strategies because most of them offer instant relief, but they offer no long-term solutions.

Making Sense of Your Current Strategies

The first step to proper stress management is to examine how you respond to stress. What are your default settings when faced with discomfort? Only once you've done this can you work toward changing the way you manage your responses. Consider journaling daily for a week or two to record your responses in real-time. Record every coping mechanism you use when you feel uncomfortable, such as eating when you're not hungry. Perhaps, you impulsively bought new shoes after your boss was a little harsh with you. Maybe you threw yourself into a new project when your spouse mentioned a topic they have been wanting to discuss for months now. Watch out for anger outbursts, and write down every detail of what happened.

You want to figure out whether these responses are good for you or not. You lashed out at James after you opened your utilities bill because it doubled since he moved in. Remember to record every detail so that you know what led up to the maladaptive coping strategy when you drank enough wine to suffer from a hangover. You want to write down every time you lit up a cigarette after a colleague made a snide comment. Keep journaling until you have a week to review at a time. Continue the exercise for another week if you find yourself using more than five of these strategies daily. Once you've identified the maladaptive strategies you use when you're stressed out, you can work on improving your stress management with new coping tools.

Chapter 4:

How to Respond to Stress

Coping mechanisms becoming habits is the good news you can use to establish new stress management tools with practice and persistence. The ball is in your court now, and all you need is to use healthy coping mechanisms to design a better stress management strategy that benefits your life, health, happiness, relationships, and performance. Fortunately, there are more healthy options, and they only need practice. Some are easy to implement in an emergency, and others will help you decrease your stress in the long run. Let's dive into the deep end of advantageous stress management.

Emergency Helpers

Stress and the management thereof are as unique as you are, so not every method works for everyone. The best emergency stress reducers can be implemented anywhere at any time, take minimal practice, provide instant relief, and don't cost a cent. What matters is that you defuse the stress response at the moment it wants to ignite. Ten emergency diffusers work wonders and some can even be combined.

The first diffuser is to slow your rushing thoughts by counting to ten before you speak or react to any stressful situation. Use the Mississippi counting strategy to regain your focus.

The second diffuser is to draw deep and slow breaths until your muscles release some of the building tension. Breathe in slowly through your nose, and push it out gently from the mouth. Imagine the air you're breathing in is peaceful, and the air you exhale is pushing the tension out. Watch your belly rise and fall as you continue breathing, paying attention to your breath and how it makes you feel.

The third diffuser is to take a quick break or walk. Remember not to avoid the situation, so keep it short. Walk to the next room so that you can briefly release the tension in the room, and take a few moments to think before responding to someone.

The fourth diffuser is to sleep on it if there's no urgency. Sometimes, this is the best strategy when you're being trolled on social media or you received a negative email.

The fifth diffuser is to walk away from your stressful situation long enough to give everyone a chance to calm down, which is especially useful in relationship conflicts. Mention that you're taking a break for an hour, and you can discuss this when you're both calmer.

Don't allow your friend to think you're avoiding the discussion.

The sixth diffuser is to break the situation or problem into smaller steps. Sometimes, it's the magnitude or volume of a problem that overwhelms you. Divide the project your boss dumped on you into four steps to make it seem less stressful.

The seventh diffuser is to turn up the volume on an inspirational song or podcast. Make sure it's positive and mood-inspiring. This tactic helps in the case of road rage when someone cuts you off.

The eighth diffuser is to take a break to redirect your mindset to something beneficial, such as petting your dog, hugging your loved ones, or helping someone with a productive or meaningful task. Hugging someone or cuddling your pet is amazingly calming and can bring your stress levels down quickly. A hormone called oxytocin is released with physical contact, and this is often referred to as the love or cuddle hormone (Scott, 2006). It can reduce blood pressure, inhibit stress hormones, and cause relaxation.

The ninth diffuser is to close your eyes and take a short vacation in your mind with some guided imagery. Imagine yourself in your happy place, and pay attention to the senses by imagining your feet in the sand, the wind whispering in your ears, and your skin feeling rejuvenated under the warm kiss of the sun. Paint a mental vacation that brings you calmness and relaxation to diffuse the onset of stress. Keep your mental vacation alive for at least a minute. You can also listen to a guided session on an app like Headspace if you find this hard to practice alone.

The tenth diffuser is to become aware of the situation and how your mind wants to respond to it. You can do this by asking yourself two questions. What are you feeling right now, and why are you feeling this way? These answers will help you recognize valuable information that needs to change in the situation or your life so that you can reconsider your options before responding to the stressor.

The bonus diffuser is to laugh or smile in the face of stress. Humor has many benefits, including bringing people closer to each other and building resilience. Be careful not to laugh at your partner's face when they're talking about something important to them. You don't want them to think you don't empathize with their concerns, even if they want a child and you aren't ready. However, laughing or smiling is a quick method for tricking the brain into believing that the stressor isn't as stressful as it thinks. So, your toddler just colored your work presentation in with crayons. Stop for a moment and laugh before you respond. Admittedly, it's funny. Lashing out at your toddler only increases your stress. Laugh about it first, and then you can consider solutions, whether it's a timeout or lost privileges.

These emergency coping mechanisms are swift, and many of them take less than a minute. Best of all is that they don't require much effort or practice.

Building Long-Term Resilience

Emotional resilience is an innate trait, but it needs to be developed and mastered, which takes time. You already possess some resilience, but you want to become the master of your emotions. It allows you to deal with stress, learn from it, and grow from the lessons hidden within it. Resilience is your ability to bounce back from negative or adverse situations and to turn them into positive developments. You should keep a journal to help maintain your awareness and acceptance of life's challenges and to apply the upcoming changes so that you appreciate them more. It provides a record of what you faced, what the hidden lesson could be, and how you can respond differently so that stress becomes your puppet. Having an internal locus of control is part of being resilient, and you can take back control of the situation when you plan the right steps forward.

Let's take an example of a mother with a toddler throwing a tantrum in a supermarket to see resilience in action. She accepts that the behavior is stressful, but what does she do to change it? She uses one of the emergency diffusers to gather herself first, and then she considers her options. She could leave the supermarket, including all of her needed groceries, or she can take her child out to the parking lot to calm him down before they return. The first option doesn't help much because she needs milk and eggs. The second option might cost her additional time, but the purpose of her shopping trip remains intact. Her options even include steps, such as taking the toddler to the parking lot to calm him down. Her plan is realistic and concrete, meaning that she can take action now. The mechanisms used by this mom was acceptance, taking control of her response, considering realistic solutions, and implementing them. The more this mom practices this quick redirection of her stress response, the more resilient she becomes, making her responses automatic when she faces the same situation again.

Unfortunately, you will face adversity, and resilience allows you to choose how you'll manage it. Challenges are a part of life. Learn to adapt to new challenges as they come, and the experience you gain in successfully diffusing and redirecting it will become your resilience. You don't only want to survive difficult situations. You want to soar above the challenge because you're in control of the outcome. Feed your experience with resilience by adopting new skills and strategies to see what changes take place. Some strategies might not help, and that's okay. Your perseverance outshines the failures when you succeed in reducing your emotional burdens with practice. Adopting a few resilience boosters can also help you succeed with emotional control.

Resilience booster one is to prioritize and find a purpose in the desired outcome. The mom's purpose was to complete her necessary shopping and reduce the stress caused by her screaming toddler. Always ask yourself what the desired outcome looks like.

Resilience booster two is to organize, manage, and structure your approach to the situation if ambiguity exists. The mom wouldn't have calmed her toddler down in the middle of the supermarket if planning was amiss.

Resilience booster three is to set and preserve boundaries. Before taking her toddler to the parking lot, the mom explained what the options were. They would either sit outside until they're calm, or they'd return home without milk for his favorite cereal.

Resilience booster four is to manage your energy and practice self-compassion. Sometimes, a stressful situation doesn't need a response. Reserve your energy for the stressful situations that need it by choosing your battles carefully. Consider whether the situation impacts your life. If not, you're fighting the wrong battle.

Resilience is also mastered through self-acceptance, proper emotional management, being optimistic, and having social support. Doctor Janine Clayton from the National Institutes of Health (n.d.), explains that resilience can help you enjoy and appreciate life, your social network, and matters that exceed your stress more. A few changes are needed to guarantee resilience.

Change Your Mindset

Reframing your mind and attitude to adopt an optimistic outlook on these stressful situations is how you can further encourage resilient growth. Optimism helps you regain your locus of control, reducing stress. Having an optimistic attitude allows you to accept the fact that you don't need to know all the answers. You only need to know who or where you can turn to for assistance. Start looking at adversity through a different lens, which is also called cognitive reframing. Start looking for alternative thoughts and emotions when you feel overwhelmed. Your employer demands that you work overtime. Look at the bright side. You'll earn more money to enjoy life on your terms. Another example is when you get stuck in a traffic jam. This is stressful to everyone involved, so look for positive benefits to your predicament.

You can listen to your favorite music, continue an audiobook you started three months ago, or you can play a game with your kids. You also need to consciously reduce your anger toward other people when they're rude or aggressive. You don't know what's happening in their lives, and that's what you need to consider. Considering multiple perspectives allows you to keep yours under control. The person might be rude because they're going through a divorce. The sight of you and your happy children reminds them how stressed they are about losing their kids. It doesn't excuse their behavior, but you can only control your behavior, so keep it positive.

Apply Positive Self-Talk

Unknowingly, we can break our resilience by talking negatively toward or about ourselves. The subconscious mind listens to this chatter, and it becomes true when you repeatedly tell yourself that you can't do something. Resilient people use positive self-talk by saying they can do it. Your thoughts have great power over your behavior and outcome, so make sure you're using positive self-talk to encourage your triumph over stress. It's an essential part of self-compassion. Learn to manage your emotions and maintain a positive outlook on adversity by practicing positive self-talk daily. Use affirmations spoken aloud in front of a mirror every morning. Think about your challenges for the day, whether they're at work, home, or in your social life. Whatever your fears manifest in the form of exaggerated thoughts are what you want to contradict. Choose five challenges daily, and weave new thoughts into your mind.

When your inner dialogue tells you that you can't do this, respond by saying: "I'm going to do the best I can because I'm in control of the situation."

When your inner dialogue tells you that everything will go sideways, respond by saying: "Taking one step at a time brings me closer to the outcome I desire."

When your inner dialogue reminds you how much you hate it when this happens, respond by saying: "I'm fortunate enough to have experience with this situation, so I have the advantage to deal with it successfully."

When your inner dialogue tells you how alone and helpless you feel, respond by saying: "I have friends and family who I can reach out to if I need help."

When your inner dialogue tells you that you're a failure, and it makes you question how you managed to screw things up so badly, respond by saying: "I'm only human with bones and skin, making me capable of mistakes like anyone else. I can and will do better next time."

Allowing your inner dialogue to direct your narrative is to give it full control. One last trick to use when you hear the inner critic is to consider what you would say to your best friend if they were in your boat. It's not about being aggressive toward the inner critic, either. It's about showing compassion and allowing the evidence to speak for itself. Sure, you'll struggle to convince yourself to just do it if you have no experience, but you can't gain experience unless you try.

Use Social Support

Many people who suffer from stress disorders have internalized their thoughts and feelings, but communicating your struggles to your social group makes a huge difference. Sometimes, all you need is to verbalize your fears, stresses, and anxieties. Talking to the right person can also help you gain insight into varying perspectives. Let's say that you're having problems at home. The anticipation of divorce can cause mountains of stress. Speak to a trusted friend or counselor who can help you look at your situation from various angles. Be honest about what led up to the situation from your perspective. Perhaps, you've grown distant because you don't know how to cope between work and the kids. Your partner also works, and the kids are demanding. The tension grew because neither of you have time to spend on your relationship. Work matters because you need money, and your children can't make themselves invisible at your request.

However, your friend suggests that you and your partner take one night a week to yourselves. She recommends her niece to babysit, which only costs half of what regular babysitters do. Talk to your social support network because they might enlighten you about options you overlooked. Besides, sharing your troubles automatically slashes them in half. Saying them out loud might even help you realize that they aren't as frightening as you thought. Heck, you could even burst out laughing at the absurdity of what you thought was impossible when a friend points to a solution. You aren't a machine, so don't treat yourself as such. Seek support from the social network you're closest to. In a worst-case scenario where you feel incapable of sharing your stress, there's nothing wrong with writing it down. Journaling your thoughts and fears could also help you see a different perspective when you revisit it. Moreover, it provides an emotional outlet.

Adopt Acceptance

According to Psychologist Erin Olivo, acceptance is the ability to reduce stress rather than to generate it (Olivo, 2015). It's another essential part of being resilient when you're experiencing distress. The reason why acceptance has so much power to change your perspective is that you learn to acknowledge stress for what it is—an emotion or perception, which stirs your thoughts and behaviors. Emotions are like children, and they'll throw tantrums, growing louder by the minute if you ignore them. Stress isn't the traffic you're stuck in, and it's not the friend who needs to chat about a broken promise. It's the emotion an object, situation, or person stirs inside of you, which changes your perception if you don't accept it. Learning to accept the emotion is the only way you allow it to run its course so that it dissipates.

Resisting stress only amplifies its discord in your life. Acceptance allows you to stop focusing solely on everything wrong so that you can also pay attention to your other thoughts, feelings, and sensations, which enables you to see a larger picture. Acceptance is your attitude and understanding, it's not an action or behavior. It leads to avoidance coping as a behavior. You develop a new state of mind when you practice acceptance. In practice, you'd recognize the cause of your stress, acknowledge that it exists, including the emotions you feel, and allow it to exist until it dissipates. Once gone, you're focused enough to deal with the situation that caused stress because the emotion was removed from the equation. When you feel stressed, tell yourself that you can't change it right now. You don't have an eraser to remove it, but you can wait for the tantrum-throwing child to reduce naturally so that your rational mind can approach the situation without emotional influence. Some situations present confusion though.

Being diagnosed with cancer doesn't mean you must accept your fate. Fate has nothing to do with your control of outcomes. You should always be realistic. You'll feel stressed along with many other negative emotions after your diagnosis. It doesn't mean you must accept death as the only outcome. You're simply accepting the emotions, which in this case, are only natural. Accepting them for what they are, which is a response to bad news will help you to see past the 'fate' fallacy. You can still live your life to the fullest of your abilities, but ignoring your emotions will only make you ruminate on the undesired outcome. The right understanding of acceptance is when you're angry at your partner. Lashing out at them does no good, but accepting that your emotions belong to you is what allows you to handle the situation without ending the relationship. Passivity and acceptance aren't the same things, either. Acceptance is a choice or perspective you choose to adopt.

Practicing acceptance is like placing the emotion and situation on a shelf while you gather your logic and calm to manage them better. It's a key part of mindfulness, so you'll learn how to practice it better in the next chapter.

Learn to How Respond to Stressful People

Let's face it, stress comes from people much of the time. Well, your perception and response to their behaviors are what instigates stress. According to Psychologist Mark Stibich, learning to effectively manage stressful people is no easy task, but it's essential to build resilience (Stibich, 2020). Removing toxic people from your life is a great method of managing stress, but you also can't remove everyone because your social support network will likely shrink. The beauty of learning how to respond to stressful people is that you most probably know them. This allows you to proactively decide how you want to handle them before tensions rise. The secret is to plan your response and stick to it. It also helps to question why you care about their behavior because a careless person has a lot of power. You can control your reaction by knowing why their behavior bothers you in the first place.

Once you're interacting with them, be careful of them pulling you onto an emotional rollercoaster. Talk, listen, and communicate without allowing them to activate negative emotions. Don't share their anger or sadness during their story. This doesn't mean that you must avoid empathy, but don't ride their emotional waves. Their emotions belong to them, and yours belong to you. You must know what you need from the interaction. Go into the conversation with a goal in mind. What do you want from it? Would you like the conversation to confirm weekend plans, but your friend won't stop complaining about their job? Keep your objective in mind, and redirect the conversation back to your original goal. The conversation will ebb and flow but stay in control of your emotions while you redirect it. If you can reach your goal during this conversation by establishing actionable weekend plans, it means you've met your goals, which also means that you've regained some control over this stressful relationship.

Make sure you don't dwell on the interaction if it went bad, either. Do your best to improve the relationship if you made a mistake, or move on if the person isn't worth saving, and whatever you do, don't allow this interaction to ruin your day.

Take Breaks

Even if you were a machine, you'd still need to enjoy rejuvenating breaks to prevent yourself from overheating and falling apart. Emotional resilience requires you to be at your peak state, and you can only do this if you're ready with buckets of energy. Burnout is a genuine threat, and you'll suffer from additional stress when you don't have enough energy to deal with incoming stress. Review your time management weekly to ensure that you're getting enough downtime. What you do in this time is entirely up to you.

Look for Lessons

Many failures, obstacles, and adversities have a lesson hidden like a gem. Pause and observe your situation to prevent stress from overwhelming you when you feel the tension set in. Does it have anything valuable to teach you? You must be objective, so pretend like you're in the position of your closest friends, and take a step back. Each friend argues about what this lesson could teach you. How will it alleviate the pressure you feel? For example, you might be stressed about missing a mortgage payment. Indeed, this is stressful, but it's not apocalyptic. Your first friend might mention the possibility that you're struggling to maintain the payments, which in a lesson is a reason for you to rent the spare room. Your second friend reminds you that this might've happened because you procrastinated on a deal at work that would have achieved the promotion you desired. This lesson inspires you to pursue the promotion now. Anyway, use the imagined friends' to look for lessons objectively so that you can take control of stressful situations and become resilient.

Getting Professional Help

There's nothing to be ashamed of if you're not coping with your stress. Stress won't vanish on its own. You'll need the tools mentioned here to manage it without risking the potential consequences of unhealthy management, but sometimes, you need a little more help. The day you're struggling to function as normal or you feel like you're drowning under stress, please speak to a professional. Don't wait for them to bring it up. They're doctors, not psychics. Seeking help from a mental health professional is perfectly normal. They've studied for years to help you when you can't manage your stress alone. If you experience the inability to control addictive behaviors, such as alcoholism and drug use, please seek immediate help. Suicidal thoughts are also cause for immediate intervention, and no one will judge you. You can call the 24-hour National Suicide Prevention Lifeline at 1-800-273-8255. However, your general practitioner can also put you in contact with the nearest resources, which includes free services. Please call when you feel like life has become too much and you have no options.

Chapter 5:

The Power of Mindfulness

Mindfulness has been trending for some time now, but its roots are from ancient practices. Chances are you've heard of the powerful tool in conversation or headlines at some point. Mindfulness is a lifestyle, attitude, and physical practice, which has been examined by modern science to help Western cultures use the same incredible means to reduce stress and many other complications from it. Learning how to be mindful in your daily life comes with a myriad of benefits, and it's not complicated. Let's explore how you can use it to cope with stress.

Mindfulness Explained

Mindfulness is achieved by training your mind-body connection with various techniques to help you remain in the present. The present moment is the most intriguing, exciting, relaxing, and rational place to exist. It's the most precious time you can experience because it's the only one that exists in reality. Mindfulness helps you live in the present, which reduces the rumination of yesterday's worries and the fears of tomorrow's possibilities. Yesterday doesn't exist in your present timeline. Indeed, it causes pain and stress that follows you around like a shadow, but what happened yesterday is over. Tomorrow is anyone's game. You might be concerned about what to expect tomorrow, but there's no guarantee that your expectations will manifest. The only evidence of yesterday and tomorrow are the feelings and thoughts you possess, even if they're not tangible or guaranteed. The techniques provided in this chapter teach you how to cope with the thoughts and feelings.

The evidence behind mindfulness continues to grow in its efficacy to reduce stress and anxiety, improve memory and attention, and help its lifestyle enthusiasts to develop self-regulation and empathy. It reduces stress because a trained mind is capable of paying attention to better protect you. Self-regulation improves because you become aware of your thoughts and feelings without judgment. You develop an open attitude to accept your stress, which allows you to tolerate it, and your mindset changes to a positive and less-reactive type. Repetitive negative thinking becomes history, and you develop a new relationship with experiences to enjoy every moment of life. According to research by the University of Minnesota, mindfulness provides boundless advantages (Delegran & Evans, 2014). The amygdala, which is the emotional center of your brain, is reduced, and the higher-thinker, rational mind, or prefrontal cortex is expanded in meditators. This means that your fearful reactivity is reduced because higher cognition is used more than emotional reasoning.

The hippocampus is where the hypothalamus part of your HPA axis exists, and this region also changes during mindfulness training, which encourages self-regulation. Mindful living improves self-awareness, emotional processing, and increased optimism. According to Psychologist Arielle Silverman from the University of Washington, there are numerous other benefits (Silverman, 2012). Mindfulness training works as well as antidepressants, and it can even reduce the complications of chronic stress, such as hypertension, heart disease, and autoimmune disorders. A mindful lifestyle can help you cope better with physical pain, lose weight, and enhance your overall mental performance. The advantages outweigh the practice you need to implement with the strategies.

Becoming mindful isn't difficult if you follow simple techniques. Keep the four cornerstones of mindfulness in mind, which are awareness, focus, acceptance, and observation. Be consciously aware of your environment, bodily sensations, feelings, thoughts, and your five senses. Be focused on the present moment. Accept and acknowledge the way you feel without judgment, and observe the changes in your environment, inside and outside. You'll learn to connect with your thoughts and feelings while being consciously aware of your surroundings. The acronym STOP is the easiest mindful trick to use in the face of stress.

- Slow down
- Take an even breath
- Observe
- Proceed

When something triggers your stress response, slow down before reacting, take even breaths to calm down, observe the situation and the environment for clues to better manage the situation, and proceed with your action plan.

If you continue to struggle with mindful training alone, consider a few more options. The mindfulness-based stress reduction (MBSR) program developed by Jon Kabat-Zin is the most popular and researched program to teach you how to live mindfully. You can find MBSR instructors online, or you can search for in-person groups in your state. You might even find training programs at your local hospital. Smartphone apps like *Headspace*, *The Mindfulness App*, or *Simply Being* are also useful when you need guidance on your meditations and breathing exercises. An important fact is that mindfulness takes practice and persistence. Don't give up after the first attempt. It could take up to six weeks to master the lifestyle.

Breathing Exercises

Mindful breathing is one of the fastest methods to calm yourself down when you feel stressed. Controlling your breath allows the mind and body to relax naturally so it's better prepared for the stress response by creating an even flow of oxygen to the brain. Three techniques can be used:

The first technique is a simple deep-breathing exercise.

- Start your exercise by making yourself comfortable on a bed or chair.
- Take a long, gentle, and even breath in through your nose, and pay attention to the way it makes your body feel.
- Hold the air for a second as you continue focusing on your body and how the air tickles your inner pathway.
- Press the air out gently, evenly, and with a little emphasis as you move your attention to the air leaving your mouth. Focus on the stress leaving your body as the air exits your system.
- Repeat this 10 times or more until you feel relaxed.

The second breathing exercise is called alternate nostril breathing. This method is best used over a few minutes or longer. It reverses the effects of stress and focuses the mind on relaxing breath that moves in and out of your alternating nostrils.

- Begin your exercise by sitting comfortably and placing your index finger against your forehead. Your thumb should rest over your nostrils.
- Push down on the right nostril, and take a slow and even breathe while you count to three.
- Hold the air for a count of two, and move your thumb to your left nostril to press it closed.
- Gently press the air out of your right nostril for three seconds.
- Take another slow and even breath into the right nostril while counting to three, and hold it for two seconds.
- Switch your thumb back to the right nostril to open your left nostril again, and press the air out gently for three seconds.
- Keep alternating between your nostrils for five minutes.

The final breathing exercise is called belly breathing. Belly breathing allows the oxygen to travel to the brain and your deepest core while you pay attention to the rise and fall of your hand. This helps you acknowledge sensational and body changes while you relax.

- Always begin your breathing exercises in a comfortable state, but this one is best if you sit on the floor with your legs crossed. Use a chair if this isn't easy for you.

- Place your left hand on your belly below your ribcage and the right hand on your chest while you close your eyes.
- Draw an even and deep breath into your nose as you pay attention to your hands resting on their focal points.
- Focus on the left hand as it rises more than the right hand, and release the breath slowly and gently again. Feel the fall of your belly as the air leaves through your mouth.
- Repeat this 10 times or more and pay close attention to how your body starts relaxing.

Progressive Muscle Relaxation (PMR)

PMR is a great way to exercise the control you have over muscle relaxation. Practice will help you recognize tension faster and release it before it turns you into a stiff deer in headlights. You should feel a sweeping relaxation throughout your body by the end of it. The secret is to focus on one muscle group at a time and pull the muscles tight before quickly releasing them.

- Make yourself as comfy as you can, whether you're lying down or sitting in a cushy chair. Close your eyes and practice your deep breathing exercise for two minutes.

- You'll already feel a lighter sensation in your muscles after deep breathing, but now you can move your focus to your forehead.
- Pull your face so that your muscles feel tense, and hold this pose for three seconds.
- Release your face muscles abruptly, and pay close attention to the tightness that leaves them.
- Move your attention down to your shoulders and neck, and pull your shoulders up high.
- Hold your position for three seconds, and let it go abruptly again, focusing on the way your muscle groups push the tension out.
- Move your fists away from your body, and pull them tight to create tension that runs into your upper arms, and hold it for three seconds.
- Release your fists swiftly, and pay attention to the changes as the tightness leaves your muscles.

Continue doing this with each muscle group until you end with your toes. Taking a deep breath is how you create temporary tension in your chest region, and pulling your toes into a ballerina position can tighten your leg and toe muscles at once. Feel free to work with each group more than once if you need to. You can also work your way back to the forehead when you're done with your first cycle. The only warning is that you don't tense aching muscle groups. Skip the right foot if you have ankle sensitivity.

Mindful Detachment

Mindfulness allows you to detach from thoughts and feelings that create misconceptions so that you can release the attachments that hold power over a situation. Mindful detachment is a process with which you consciously let go of attachments to clear your mind. This allows you to detach yourself from unwanted thoughts and processing. Understand that thoughts are only thoughts, and they have no tangible connection to reality or the present moment. To practice mindful detachment in your daily life, close your eyes and imagine the stressor being just a thought. It's a passing notion that might change. Imagine a scenario that causes stress, whether it's a goal or a person. What makes you feel incomplete if you don't have your desired outcome? Let's say that you want to receive a compliment from a certain someone today.

For what reason would the failure to achieve this compliment stand in your way of being whole? Is it fear, anger, or maybe vanity? Consider whether this attachment has anything to do with your overall happiness. If not, you've recognized an attachment for what it is—a preconception that everything must go your way or you won't be happy. Allow your imagined situation to play out in your mind, and realize whether this single, tiny incident can truly make you feel whole. Mindful detachment is an observation, which allows you to look at something you think you want from a different perspective. It also familiarizes you with uncertainty and allows you to stop beating yourself up for nothing. Moreover, you'll familiarize yourself with the authentic person who lives inside of you.

Meditation

The human mind's ability to wander into timelines that don't exist is phenomenal. Many people prefer to live in the past or future because the present offers a challenge; however, their wandering minds take them to timelines that cause distress. Meditation is the most valuable commodity of the MBSR program, and it has key benefits for your health according to Harvard Medical School (Mineo, 2018). Neuroscientist Sara Lazar documented the changes in grey matter in the brain, proving that meditation is the key technique to reduce stress and regulate your emotions. In fact, it can switch the relaxation response on. Harvard is one of many universities offering meditation training now, focusing mainly on mindful meditation, which allows people to increase their awareness of their thoughts, prevent immediate responses, and grow compassionately aware of their body and mind. You also develop compassion toward other people, change your perception of stress, and develop emotional resilience.

Training yourself in mindful meditation requires practice and consistency. The reason why people fail is that they give up before they develop new habits. A daily practice over six weeks brings immense benefits, and it can be as simple as starting with 10 minutes a day. However, the recommended time to achieve the greatest benefits with the MBSR program is to practice it twice daily for 20 minutes. Mindful meditation also requires a focal point, which could be a mantra you adopt during your practice. You might repeat a number, such as one, or you can use classical mantras that elongate the vowel, such as 'om.' A mantra can also be the repetition of the word 'calm.' Simply elongate the word. You could also use meditation to remain present and practice mindfulness, or you can use focal points by using your senses, such as touch, smell, sight, sound, and taste. Some people simply focus on their breath.

The secret to mindful meditation is that you pay attention to your focal point and bring your attention back to it when your mind wanders off. You also aren't allowed to judge yourself for wandering off. The best position to practice meditation in is called the easy yoga pose, which requires sitting on a cushion on the floor, crossing your legs, and holding your palms in an upward lotus position, but you can do it in a chair to start with. Comfort is the key because discomfort offers a distraction. Follow these simple guided sessions to begin your training.

Letting Go

The "letting go" technique is a great first practice for mindful meditation. Position yourself as you feel cozy, and close your eyes as you pay attention to your breathing. Don't even attempt to control the air moving in and out. Simple focus on it, and pay attention to how your body feels while you spend two minutes in this state.

Notice how the air makes your throat feel as it passes through to your belly, and follow it back out before drawing another one. Feel your body moving as you continue breathing gently and evenly. There's no rush to where you're going. Just be you, and you're in this present space and time, focusing on the movement of your body as you breathe.

Thoughts and emotions will come to pass. Allow them to float around your present space. Pay attention to your thoughts as they move through your mind while you take another breath. Observe the way each emotion changes the way your calming body feels, and consciously let it go now. You're not judging it or being unkind to it.

Take another deep and slow breath as another thought stirs. Observe it as it slowly grows weaker and weaker before you let it go. Let go of every thought that passes through your mind, without allowing them to take your attention away from your breathing. These thoughts and emotions want to distract you, but let them go.

Every time your mind wanders to another feeling or idea, let them go and bring your attention back to your present breathing. Thoughts keep streaming into your line of attention, but your conscious decision to return your focus to your breath allows you to let them go. Fear wants to pop into your mind, allow your breathing to let it go.

Reminders of a time gone by want to disturb your peaceful present moment. Let them go as you draw another breath and focus carefully on it. Whatever you do, keep noticing the sensations in your body as your breath combs through your belly and throat. The peaceful presence of your controlled breathing is making you calmer and more focused.

The calmness becomes you, allowing you to let go of another fear that belongs to tomorrow. Slowly and gently, press the air out of your mouth while recognizing the sensations, and let go of your fear. Nothing is allowed in your present space but your breathing and the calming sensations that follow.

You've never felt this relaxed before, and you're slowly gaining the control to let go of any thoughts or emotions that come. Before you know it, the only things that remain are you and your breathing. Nothing else exists anymore but calmness and peace. Remain in this state for some time, and allow the calmness to overcome you.

Mindful Decluttering

Bring yourself to your most comfortable position before you close your eyes once more. The time has come to declutter the sensations causing you discomfort. Start with an even breath in through the nose, allow it to circulate in your lowest belly, and push it out slowly. Take another deep breath, trying to reach a deeper part of your belly this time.

Don't force the air too hard, but draw it gently into your core. Follow the breath as it warmly embraces the pathway to the core. You can feel each touch of breath as it comes back through your nose. Take a few more breaths, following each one to the core, paying attention to every embrace along the way.

Repeat your cycle in and out until you feel your muscles melting ever so slightly. The air coming in brings warmth and calmness while the air passing out is providing an exit for the tension you feel. Once you feel calm enough, allow your thoughts and emotions to visit your present space. Permit them to join you so that you can acknowledge them.

Draw another warm and peaceful breath as a distressing emotion enters your space. Use your calming presence in the present moment to establish your control over your reaction to this fear. Your mind and body are relaxed. You can control your brain to not respond to the concern. Simply observe the fear as it passes through your mind and into your body.

Follow it until it reaches a physical space. Perhaps, it lies over your heart now. Accept that this fear is passing through your present timeline, and allow it to just be. Give it a physical shape and volume so that it knows you're paying attention to it. Notice the sensations around it, and keep drawing warm, gentle breaths that circulate the fear.

Each breath takes one more piece of the fear away. The fear slowly shrinks with each breath that brings comfort and the recognition of the present moment. Your breath is slowly dwindling the fear. The fear exists, and you acknowledged it, but it's dissipating before your inner eyes. Take a final breath to shrink it down to nothingness.

Your fear was real, but it can't live in the present with you. It can only pass through, and you can allow it to dissipate as you observe it without judgment or force. Repeat your breathing cleanse if you notice more thoughts and feelings that need to pass. They can't pass out of your present time unless you pay attention to them.

Be gentle, kind, and loving to yourself while you continue this session. Once you open your eyes, sit in the stillness that is your present time, and absorb the sensations of relaxation and calmness before returning to the flow of life.

Additional Mindful Activities

Mindfulness encourages you to establish a connection with the present moment, and you can easily do this by using your five senses. Mindful eating is another activity you can use every time you eat. Quite simply, pay attention to the senses while you eat something. Take an apple as an example. Don't just gush it down. Eat it slowly, focusing on the crunchiness as your teeth sink through the skin, the cracking sound it makes, and the taste of tiny, morsels dancing on your tongue. Watch how the shape of it changes as you take another bite, and recognize how bright the skin is. Pay attention to the smell as you bite into it once more. The same mindful technique can be used for any food, even ice cubes, and drinks. Try to focus on how each sense ignites as you partake in mindful eating.

Mindful movements are another way for you to establish your present moment connection. Don't just take a walk through the forest. Feel the movements of your body as you connect to the ground, and how this connection changes the sensations in your leg muscles. Feel each foot hit the ground, and pay attention to the release when you raise it. Focus on your breathing, how it changes, and how it makes your body feel as you jog. Listen to its whispers, and give some attention to your surroundings. Use your senses to listen to the birds singing their daily songs, smell the fresh air and flowers, and look at the amazing creatures scurrying away from the path. Feel the temperature changes on your skin as you go between shade and sun, and keep focusing on your present experience in the forest. Tai Chi is a gentle martial art that helps you train your mindful movement by repeating slow movements in sync with other people.

Body scans are also a popular meditation practice in mindfulness. Use breathing exercises to bring yourself to a calmer state before the session. Much like combining the PMR technique with the decluttering meditation session, you'll scan your body for tension and unwanted feelings. Similar to giving your fear space in your timeline during the decluttering session, you'll start at one end of your body and move to the other end as you did in PMR, except you don't need to tense your muscles. Body scan meditations aren't controlling. They're simply observational so that you can acknowledge your feelings, give them physical forms, and allow yourself to detach from them. Focus your attention on one area at a time, and recognize any discomfort in the region. Be gentle and kind so that the discomfort passes before you move on to the next region. You aren't allowed to react to them or judge them. Use the reverse method by starting with your toes, focusing on your legs and torso, and working your way up to your forehead. Give each region a few moments to identify discomfort, and move on when the discomfort no longer pains you.

Loving-kindness meditation is another exercise you can practice. In this meditation, you'll also make yourself comfortable, close your eyes, and use a breathing exercise to bring calmness over yourself for a minute before you spread the love. Where does love start though? It's impossible to have affection for others if you don't care for yourself, so loving-kindness meditation starts with you. In a calm state, imagine yourself as another person standing in front of you. Give this person a few compliments to boost their well-being. Be kind and gentle to them, and allow them to smile before you move to the next person. Replace your imagined self with your closest loved ones, and share kindness with them. Then, you can replace them with people in your community so that you can share the love with a wider group of people. You're only allowed to share positive thoughts, feelings, and compliments with everyone. This meditation type helps you establish positive feelings toward yourself and others when you feel distressed.

Yoga is undeniably a great mindfulness practice. It's an effective training tool you can adopt from a masterful instructor if you join the right class. It combines breathing exercises with mindful movements, light exercise, and meditation. It's a combination of mindful practices that offer fun as well. However, it requires a frequent routine, such as twice weekly. Don't expect miracles from one session. Moreover, learning and holding the poses help you connect to the present moment. It gives you something to focus on while your body and mind are being engulfed in mindfulness. Yoga is great for mental and physical health, but you should consider signing up for a class first to ensure proper training. There are also various types of yoga, so be sure to check whether your class offers deep breathing, stretching, and slow movements, which are the best for reducing stress and anxiety.

The final technique to mention is aromatherapy. Essential oils are made of many plants that offer relaxation, but they have vast benefits. The essential oils used in aromatherapy activate smell receptors in your nose, which directly communicate with your brain through the nervous system (Pagan, 2018). This explains why aromatherapy is a mindful practice because it uses your sense of smell to make changes in the brain. Areas activated by the oils include the limbic system, which plays a role in emotional regulation, and the hypothalamus, which then releases serotonin to induce the relaxation response. Lavender, patchouli, spearmint, and ylang-ylang are popular relaxation essential oil extracts. Place a few around your home. You can also place a drop on your finger and sweep it under your nose. Essential oils also help with physical pain and tension, so rub them into your skin around painful areas. Take a bath with essential oils burning so that you double your relaxation.

Mindfulness is truly a key part of your freedom from the stress curse, but there are more daily habits you can change to increase your resilience.

Chapter 6:

Healthy Habits That Keep Stress at Bay

You're well on your way to a life with minimal stress and discomfort, but you need to ask yourself whether anything else is amiss. Take a look at your daily lifestyle, and consider whether your choices create or diminish stress. People often misunderstand that the mind and body are connected. What goes into the body can affect the mind, and what the body experiences daily can also impact your mental and emotional well-being. The connection works in the opposite direction, too. What is allowed in the mind can impact your body. A collection of new habits will take care of this predicament so that you can find freedom from stress.

Sleep Hygiene

Stress causes a lack of sleep, so chances are that you're well aware of the relationship between sleep hygiene and emotional well-being. Insomnia is a common addition of distressed individuals, especially if they lose more than three nights of peaceful sleep per week over a three month period. Insomnia also doesn't only define the inability to fall asleep. It's also the struggle to remain asleep. According to the Mayo Clinic Staff (2019b), you need between seven and nine hours of sleep daily. Otherwise, your immune system is at risk, and so is your judgment, making you more prone to have a short fuse when small stressors happen. Good sleep hygiene is what's required to ensure improved resilience. A few habit changes can improve your chances of sleeping better. Make sure your bedroom is dark enough, and control the temperature by setting it to between 60 and 65-degrees Fahrenheit. You also want a quiet space where noisy neighbors and traffic can't disturb your sleep.

Keep the windows shut to block out the noise, or get a white noise machine to distract your mind from outside disturbances. You can also include meditation or other relaxation exercises before bedtime. It's mostly inside noises that keep us awake when thoughts and emotions run wild. Electronics, social media, and even the television must be switched off 30 to 60 minutes before you sleep because they cause mental disruptions with blue light. Try not to even check your messages before bedtime. Stick to reading an inspirational book or take a relaxing bath before you sleep. What you do before bed matters. Avoid caffeine and alcohol before sleeping. Getting enough sunlight during the day also makes you sleep better at night, and being comfortable sure helps. Change your bed if it offers no support or comfort.

The most important part of good sleep hygiene is to keep a routine. You have a circadian rhythm, which wakes you and makes you sleepy on routine, so train the rhythm by keeping the same sleep schedule daily, even on weekends.

Become Active

Moving your body is another lifestyle change you should make. According to the Anxiety and Depression Association of America (ADAA, 2000), a mere 30 minutes of daily exercise can boost your mood and suppress negative emotions. Often, all you need is to walk outside. The reason why being active can transform your mood and benefit your health is that endorphins and endocannabinoids are released. The former hormone is a feel-good booster, and the latter inhibits pain, improves your sleep, and can even sedate you. Your self-esteem can also prevail, making life a lot easier. Breaking a sweat can be achieved with walking (brisk), running, cycling, swimming, yoga, dancing, aerobics, or signing up at a gym.

If 30 minutes sounds overwhelming, you can divide it into three sessions of 10 minutes. The only precaution you should take is that you shouldn't exercise immediately before bedtime, which could disrupt your sleep if you're experiencing a "runner's high" from the hormones. Exercise can seem daunting, but you can enlist an exercise buddy to join you, listen to music on your earphones, or find the right routine that you enjoy. If you struggle to find the time to exercise daily, you can always turn regular chores or daily habits into exercise routines. Be creative, and challenge yourself to complete your house cleaning in half the time to break a sweat. It counts, and so does cycling to the supermarket instead of driving. Choose the stairs rather than an elevator, take a scenic jog during your lunch break, wash your car, or park far away from the office door (when safe). Turn your daily life into a challenge that helps you exercise, and try to include some outdoor activities.

Eating Right

What you eat really is what you become, and it's not only about your waistline. Food impacts your mood, thoughts, sleep, fitness, and health on many levels. The relationship between food and stress is a complex one for many people because junk food, sugar, fat, and all the bad stuff is tempting when it provides comfort. The problem with modern, processed, and fast foods is that they give the brain comfort by feeding it with chemicals that promote addiction. That's how food companies maintain their competitive edge over each other. Sugary foods impact your mood because the sugar high is closely followed by the crash. Many of these modern foods promote higher blood pressure and bad cholesterol, too. These factors impact your immune system, putting you at greater risk for more stress.

You're often left with two problems. The first is that your hormones are being controlled by unhealthy foods, and the second is that your body's external physique changes, leaving you depressed and anxious. Your self-esteem isn't the winner after a binge session with junk food.

You have to change your daily eating habits, and it starts by avoiding alcohol and caffeine, which are stimulants that wire your stress hormones. Start eating complex carbohydrates that take longer to break down so that your glucose and insulin levels remain consistent. Complex carbs are found in whole grains, leafy green vegetables, quinoa, barley, and legumes, such as lentils, beans, and chickpeas. Purchase lean proteins from organic and ethically-raised animals. Healthy fats are found in fresh fish, nuts, avocados, organic meat, and free-range eggs. Antioxidants are another key ingredient to a healthy diet because they protect your cells against breakdowns caused by stress hormones. Spices like ginger, turmeric, and coarse black pepper are good sources, and antioxidants are also abundant in fruits, vegetables, and berries. Keep in mind that all your produce must be organic to avoid the chemicals in pesticides, too. Drink plenty of water, and add a few nutrients to your diet. Vitamin C, magnesium, and omega-three fatty acids should be in your daily diet.

It's not all doom and gloom though. A study published by the University of Dammam in Saudi Arabia confirmed that dark chocolate can reduce stress hormones (Al Suni & Latif, 2014). Milk chocolate is a no-go. Healthy snacks are out there, you just have to avoid the bad stuff, especially processed foods. It's also not only what you eat that impacts your health and mental well-being. It's how you eat that makes a difference. Consider eating mindfully to slow down your consumption and turn it into an experience that helps your stress in multiple ways.

Gather the Right Troops

One human fault is that we believe we're capable of carrying the world on our shoulders. Pride often stands in the way of seeking help from those who would be most willing to provide it. Leaning on the right people in times of need can make your life a lot less stressful. Humans thrive when they stand in communities because life has become too complicated and busy to face alone. Start surrounding yourself with emotionally and physically supportive friends, family, colleagues, and even spiritual leaders who can provide a positive effect on your well-being. This already increases your chances of being the resilient person you deserve to be. Moms should seek help when they feel overwhelmed in their balance between work and kids. Dads should reach out when they feel the pressure of a looming project deadline at work while they try to maintain their relationship with their partners. There's nothing quite like getting something off your chest when you feel overwhelmed, and a minister can provide a listening ear. Call a friend, and ask them to assist you with finding a new partner if you're struggling to overcome the anxiety of meeting someone new.

Gathering the right troops allows you to find even support among a community of friends and family. Build mutually supportive relationships with people, keep in touch with them, and make sure you're surrounded by practical and emotional support. The trick with mutually meaningful relationships is that you step in when they're feeling under pressure, too. A video recently went viral of a fire truck trying to reach a burning apartment, but its path was blocked by a car parked in the way. What was possibly a crowd of 20 or more people ran to the car, and believe it or not, they managed to move it enough to allow the fire engine through. You are the fire engine, and the burning apartment is your stress, so allow your close-knit community to offer the support they would love to give. Giving back to the community also helps you experience a feel-good moment like no other. Volunteer work might even help you connect with the right troops if you don't have anyone yet. The world is filled with people willing to help, including religious leaders, therapists, and caring friends, so reach out to them, and allow them to clear the path to your burning apartment.

Laugh Out Loud

Laughing is an emergency fixer for when you face stressful times, but the health benefits indicate that you should be spreading contagious humor daily (Brown, 2019). Laughter tricks the brain because the regions involved with the processing aren't capable of doing their duties without some form of instruction. The senses give the HPA axis a reason to set off your alarm, but laughter is a sudden bolt of energy that fools the brain into believing that something amazing happened. Have you ever noticed how genuine laughter can hurt your stomach muscles? That's because it's a full-on, physical attack of joy. It disrupts thoughts and emotions quickly, and the brain releases dopamine and serotonin to inhibit the stress hormones, and this release even boosts the immune system. Happier people truly are healthier. Searching for giggles is easy. Watch a few human failure videos on YouTube. There are endless videos of people doing the dumbest stuff you can imagine, but it makes you laugh. Try to have a belly-crunching laugh at least once a day.

Express Gratitude

Gratitude seems like the most distant intention when you're about to scream, but it's another habit that helps your mind change the perception of what just happened. Let's say that you're feeling wired after sitting in standstill traffic that made you late for work. Indeed, you're ungrateful for the inconvenience and tardiness; however, there are numerous reasons to be grateful. You're grateful for arriving at work safely after seeing the pileup that made you realize how many people didn't have the privilege of safety on the road this morning. You're also grateful for getting a chance to listen to your favorite radio host who had you in stitches with his silly prank. You're grateful that you woke up this morning, and you can't deny the wonderful feeling you had when your children hugged you tighter than a boa constrictor at school.

There are always more reasons to be grateful than not. Gratitude is part of being optimistic, and you force your brain to remember why stress won't define you. Express gratitude daily to make it a new habit that keeps your mind positive. Start a gratitude journal where you record three things that you're grateful for daily, and they can be anything from waking up to receiving a compliment about your new shirt. You can also practice gratitude as a family by allowing each person to say what they're most grateful for around the dinner table. Turn everyday into Thanksgiving. Gratitude can even remind you of how many resources you have to cope with stress healthily, so don't underestimate the power of appreciation.

Experience Joyful Activities

A restless mind can be calmed and soothed by an enjoyable activity. It's the most natural way for you to reduce stress and bring serenity into your daily life if you allow activities that provide moments of pleasure and laughter. Life has become a fast-paced rat race and we're all running to reach some finish line. Hardly ever do we stop and smell the flowers along the path. Our days are filled with getting the kids out of bed, which is a momentous task, followed by the struggle to get them into the car for school. Getting stuck in the morning traffic jam, juggling the responsibilities of five people while trying to get a promotion, and still having to take a break from work to pick the kids up from school, and move them to extracurricular activities is a normal day for many people. Coming home would seem like the end of it, but you have to make dinner, help with homework, and unwind after putting the kids to sleep. Just as you're about to have a deep conversation with your partner, you roll over to find them fast asleep. The effort required to wake them up is too much, so you close your eyes. It all happens again the next day, but in-between this madness, there has to be time for yourself.

Even if you only spend 15 minutes a day with yourself, doing what you love, it's enough to make a difference in a stress-filled life. The only precaution you must take during your downtime is to guarantee that the activity doesn't encourage competitiveness because this induces more stress. Find a stress-busting activity, or a few of them so that you can start enjoying your life again. Dedicate time to your freedom from the rat-race every day, and don't feel hesitant to ask for help from your support network if your kids are dangling from your arms. A childminder also works in this case, and 15 minutes won't take away your performance from work if you arrive with a fresh and calm mind the next day. Art is one option to consider. Why don't you learn to paint or play an instrument? Adult coloring is also surprisingly relaxing. Moreover, art gives you an outlet to express your emotions and thoughts. You can paint your future self as you'd like to reach your fullest potential. You could hit those keys on the piano like a punching bag to allow the music to flow your anger and frustration out. Doodle ideas, which might even bring inspiration for solutions.

Focus your mental energy on designing a scrapbook or photo album where you can reminisce on the happy memories. You can even do this with the kids. Reading, paging through a magazine, or writing short stories can also relax a restless mind. Sport is another option, and it can be a team effort that provides additional support as well. Tennis, golf, football, basketball, boxing, baseball, or any sport you enjoy are good activities as long as they don't make you competitive. Play for the heck of it, and benefit from the workout to double this stress-buster. Hobbies are also great because they allow you to reach a state of flow if you choose the right ones. You can lose track of time and forget about your worries while you build model airplanes, knit, sew, make jewelry, or join a pottery class. Sometimes, all it takes to make an activity enjoyable is the combination of doing what you love with the people you love. Play outside with the kids, or take your dog to the park. You can also listen to positive music or find inspirational speakers in your area if you like this. Take a walk in the glory of nature, remembering to do it mindfully, or soak in a bubble bath to wash your stress away.

Meditate or practice yoga in the park or any outdoor area that enhances your experience. Gardening is another great activity, and it boosts your positive mood further when you see the improvements that you're capable of making. Home improvement projects have the same benefits. Furthermore, combine your exercise routine with your enjoyable activities, and take a run or cycle through an inspiring outdoor place. The only way you can break the burden of stress is to find your groove with multiple habits, and enjoyable activities give you loads of inspiration. You deserve to laugh and smile. You deserve to have fun at least once a day.

Learn Self-Kindness

Self-kindness is not a selfish trait. It's a necessary part of being self-compassionate, and the failure to be gentle with yourself is likely to cause stress. The truth is that you have expectations, whether they were set by your parents, teachers, boss, or spouse, you have an idea of what your life should look like. The problem with your expectations is that they might not be realistic, or you may expect to become your greatest self in an unachievable timeframe. It's easier for you to criticize yourself because failing to meet your expectations is like letting yourself down. However, this describes someone who isn't kind or patient with themselves. Moreover, self-criticism is a default setting in highly-strung individuals who believe that perfectionism is the only answer. They fail to see that every human has flaws and inadequacies, but these imperfections are what make them unique. Otherwise, the world would be a boring place.

Self-kindness builds a tolerance for these imperfections so that you can see the beauty of your individuality. Being gentle with yourself gives you the tools to support yourself when you feel overwhelmed, inadequate, or like you've failed your expectations. Sometimes, you become unkind to yourself because you're not intentional or purposeful. If whatever you do is intentional and has a purpose behind it, you won't feel inadequate. Having intentional expectations can help you live by your values and interests. Ask yourself what you truly need to do at this time. What would make your stress dissipate? Keep focusing on the abundance of what you have and what you've already achieved, and stop giving power to mistakes because we all make them. You can adopt the kindest quality by letting go of expectations that can't be met. Don't hold yourself to a life of stress because you expect the sun to shine at midnight. Let go of your expectations, and enjoy the moment before it passes. Let go of self-criticism and negative self-talk, and join the flow of life that brings a positive impact.

One exercise you can practice to improve your self-kindness is role-playing. Think about the kindest person you've ever met, whether it's a relative, friend, public figure, teacher, minister, or your favorite fictional character from a great novel. Take this person's role as your own, and speak out loud to yourself when you hear the critic becoming restless. You can also do it silently in your mind if you're not alone. Pretend to sit in a chair across from this yourself, and adopt the conversation this person will have with you. Determine what words are needed in your gentle conversation. Kindness has many definitions, including patience, caring, tenderness, welcoming, giving, gratefulness, compassion, non-judgmental, warm, and understanding. Allow your imagined role-player to use these words as they soothe you during your time of distress. The tone of voice also matters. Imagine them speaking to you with the gentlest tone you've ever heard. It flows through you, bringing calmness over your restless mind. You can also imagine that you're talking to your reflection, pretending to speak to it as you would a beloved child or pet. This is the habit you need to adopt daily. You should be able to speak to yourself like the kindest person you know would.

Another self-soothing kindness exercise involves physical touch. Psychotherapist Beverly Engel explains that physical touch in any form releases oxytocin, the invaluable love hormone (Engel, 2018). Imagine the most calming embrace you've ever experienced. It might be the way your partner touches your arm when he comes home, or it can be the soothing strokes of your mother's fingers through your hair when you were a child. Perhaps, it's the soft touch of your children's hands as they grab your face to kiss you. You can replicate this feeling if you touch yourself in the same way. Don't resist it, even though you'll be hesitant because you think you can't match the embrace. Set your intentions to soothe yourself, and run your fingertips gently over your arm. Absorb the pleasures within this embrace, and talk to yourself in a nurturing voice as you keep stroking your arm. Remind yourself that you deserve to be happy, loved, and patient with yourself.

Applying daily habits to your life gives you more powerful resilience. You'll start implementing your healthy coping tools with greater ease if you're kind to yourself. Your healthy body will encourage a healthy and happy mind, and your activities give you an outlet for expression and passion. Don't underestimate your abilities, and never beat yourself up for falling short when your expectations were wrong. And if nothing else works today, find a reason to laugh until you fold over. Applying everything you've learned to your daily life seems daunting, but a little planning will do wonders.

Chapter 7:

Making Your Life Less Stressful

Using the tools that you've gathered up to this point will change your life in ways you only dreamed about; however, a lack of planning and organization can cause resistance or futility from a successful shift to a better, happier, and healthier life. In some cases, people have the skills they need to overcome their distress, but their efforts are in vain because they don't have the organizational skills added to their strategy. Learning to prioritize, eliminate, and simplify your life is part of being in control of your future outcomes. Furthermore, it's simpler than you think. Follow the 11 steps to freedom so that your life is truly void of the complications stress brings.

Step One: Plan Ahead

On what grounds do you believe that the greatest wars in history were won? Military generals, along with strategists, planned their attack and defense. They couldn't send their men onto the battlefield without a strategy in mind. Indeed, plans don't always run as we want them to, but without strategies, time management, and effective defense mechanisms, we would fall in the trenches. These military powerhouses made plans on top of plans, on top of more plans because contingency plans were the reasons why many wars didn't go the other way. It gave their soldiers effective backup plans for when the enemy broke the original one. Quite simply, you are the soldier running onto the battlefield that is everyday life, but without promoting yourself to a general or strategist, you might fall in the first line of fire. It's no secret that stress mounts when you run short of time or strategies to combat the enemy. In many cases, stress manifests when things don't go as planned because something unexpected happened. You can't account for every possible outcome, but you can have enough resources to adopt a quick contingency plan.

Stay ahead of the enemy by preparing yourself for meetings, scheduling your time for minimal impact, and creating realistic goals for the long and short run. Don't leave things for the last minute, and make sure your hours are accounted for. You can't do this if you're not following a daily calendar. Your plans should include all the stuff that makes you anxious like work and performance reviews, but it should also contain a healthy amount of you-time, enjoyable activities, and family time. Life, like any battlefield, requires a balance between rest and work. You need to find the line between fun and serious. The moment you realize that your calendar doesn't contain enough balance, or it causes you more distress and failed time-management, you need to trim the edges. We tend to perform better when we have breaks between the grinds. Make sure you have exercise, fun activities, and some unwinding moments between your busy slots throughout the day. Every soldier needs free or restful time to gather themselves before they charge into the field.

Step Two: Get Organized

Organization skills aren't innate. They require cultivation and practice. Yet, the lack of this priceless skill is the cause of much of your distress. Whether you're forgetting important dates, or you can't remember the incredible solution you came up with yesterday, your inability to organize your life can create cracks in your potential for a stress-free life. However, even the most disorganized person can learn to be better at this skill. Being able to organize your meetings so that you handle them with ease, learning to say no when someone asks you for an unrealistic favor, or organizing your time and efforts with technology and simple tricks can make a world of difference.

Whether you use an alarm clock to wake up, or you rely on a handheld digital assistant, you're already applying some organization to your life. Determine what you can control before organizing your life, and take charge of it. There will always be things you can't control, such as the school calling about your sick child, but taking control of your daily to-do list is one thing you can use to decrease the stress you experience. The most obvious way to start organizing your life is to write everything down. You can't expect yourself to remember every birthday, anniversary, deadline, shopping list item, idea, meeting, or important date, so write it down before your mind becomes overwhelmed by the mass influx of information. Carry a notebook with you to record ideas as they come because Murphy's Law says we'll forget the most valuable ones. An information overload only causes memory failure, which leads to stress when you miss an important deadline. Even your budget should be recorded on a computer to make your financial life easier.

Create deadlines and schedules for your time, which is a precious commodity that turns to anxiety when it runs out. Scheduling your time, much like planning, allows you to be productive and capable of handling more during the day because you know what's coming. Just remember to stick to your deadlines. A weekly or monthly planner helps, but stick to timeframes to make sure these tasks move off the list. Don't overwork yourself on a project so that your leisure time suffers. Consider your bucket list as another list of things you need to organize. If your timeframes are realistic, you can achieve your dreams by sticking to a schedule. Procrastination is a dangerous pitfall that could derail your organizational skills, but you won't let it happen. Any effort is better than nothing, but procrastination only moves your goalposts further away. You should also keep your task list clean and handy at all times. Having your tasks spread out over five different devices, three worksheets, and a shopping list pinned to the fridge won't help you stay organized.

It will confuse and overwhelm you when you arrive home from the supermarket after shopping with your digital list, but you forgot eggs and cereal because they were listed on the fridge. A small irritation can become a huge pain when it takes you half an hour to reach the supermarket and you need to bath the kids. Have a global device if you're going digital, or allocate a time every night where you update your online worksheets with your handwritten notes. Fortunately, smartphones have become quite handy, offering us handheld personal assistants. There are apps for shopping lists, budgeting, inspirational notes, inspirational photos for ideas, and calendars. Most people keep their phones on them, so it makes the device an omnipresent solution, even at work. Always write down your three main tasks for the next day before you go to bed, whether it's dropping the kids at school, finishing your work presentation, or buying groceries. This acts as a springboard of productivity for the next day.

Other than keeping your personal assistant close by, you should also make it easier to complete a task. Everything should have a space in your home, and it must always go back in its place when you're done with it. This helps you find and use it faster and easier next time. Organizing your life is simple with the help of smartphones and simple rules, such as putting it away right now where it belongs, and giving yourself timeframes for each task.

Step Three: Declutter

Clutter is an eye-sore for some, but others love collecting more stuff than they can use, which is called hoarding in extreme cases. Hoarding is a psychological condition, so don't sweep it under the rug. Nevertheless, compare your mind to your home for a moment. What would your mind feel like if it had as many objects lying around as your living room? Think about each object being a point of focus for you. Chances are that there are many unnecessary items, and they're stealing the living room's focus. Clutter only causes more stress when you consider how many distractions lie around and how many unfinished projects might hide between them. The evidence of a cluttered home influencing your well-being is documented (Resnick, 2018). A messy space only indicates more work in the near or distant future, and unfinished projects can tug at your attention. Let's face it, humans hate starting something and not finishing it. Living in a cluttered space leads to depression, anxiety, and stress because it also creates a sense of having no control over your environment, even if you don't recognize it.

Piles of unwashed dishes, laundry covering the bathroom floor, and paperwork is strewn across the table don't make you feel confident, either. In fact, it can be embarrassing when people come over, giving you more reasons to stress. It's also easier to focus when your home reflects how organized and intentional your life is. Removing the clutter even improves your memory, attention span, and concentration. Your sleep is another improvement made when you clean house. A shocking fact is that women are more likely to hoard, and hoarders are 77% more likely to suffer from obesity (Lowin, 2015). Decluttering your home and office can even help you maintain physical health by eating better, which also improves your mood. Start changing your situation by allocating 15 minutes a day to declutter your space. Identify items you don't need, donate what you can throw out, and box up anything that doesn't belong in your daily tasks. Pack a box for your local charity store by putting one more item in it every day, and drop it off monthly. Pay attention to how your life feels lighter as the items start disappearing.

You can also sell the items you don't need, which might even lessen the burden of financial strain. Have a garage sale where you get rid of anything that isn't necessary to become a minimalist. You should also create a decluttering checklist. Start in one part of your home, and move through it with your list to remind you not to skip forgetful corners. Stand back, and view your home as though you're visiting it as a friend if you struggle to see the problem. Make a note of how clean and organized it seems if you were pretending to be a friend. You could even ask a friend to help you. An easy system to use during your declutter exercise is the four-box system. Label the boxes as 'keep,' "throw away," 'donate,' and 'relocate.' The labels say enough. Get into your desk drawers, too. Work through your paperwork in your short spring-cleaning sessions daily. Make sure you keep important documents but throw out what collects dust.

Once your home is anew, keep it that way. Always clear the table or desk before calling it a night, and stop leaving the dishes and laundry out until next spring. Finally, declutter your laptop, desktop, and smartphone from any apps or junk that doesn't belong on the home screens. These are also distractions that steal your attention.

Step Four: Simplify

To simplify your life is to downsize from a highly-strung, fast-paced existence to a simpler one, which contains far less stress. The simplicity movement is a new trend in living with freedom from the high-octane triggers of modern life. Some people take this movement rather seriously, returning to the woods to live off the land, but this isn't necessarily what you're about to do. Indeed, you can live off the land, but simple living has nothing to do with being impoverished, ignorant, or becoming a hippy from the 1970s. It's about making life easier to live so that you don't have additional stressors when they don't need to be there. A simple lifestyle allows you to appreciate what you have more, find time for what matters, and align your goals with your values. To simplify your life, you need to start automating what you can, which you've already done in step two if you adopted a global organizer. However, you can automate more than this. You can hire a cleaning service once a week, find a reliable and trustworthy nanny to help with the kids, and move to online banking to avoid long queues. You can even schedule payments so that you don't have to log in every month.

A simple life also means that you should live within your budget. If you haven't started using a budget yet, you should. It can decrease your stress by guaranteeing that you stick to your financial plan. Just remember to be strict with yourself about the budget. Financial planning can also help you decrease your debt over time. It keeps you focused on paying off your debt while you track your repayment progress. You could use the zero-based budget, which means that you have to allocate every cent, including leisure expenses. It's easy to think we have more money when we simply haven't calculated the leisure activities. Don't put yourself under additional pressure by adopting a budget that makes you anxious, either. Go through every bill statement and income stub to balance your zero-based budget so that you don't leave yourself with obligations you can't meet. Never forget your imperfections, either. Be kind to yourself when you make mistakes because you can't live a simple life as a perfectionist. Simplifying also means that you must reduce your dependencies on people, gadgets, and outcomes that you expect to bring you joy. You can experience every moment of life without these things or people.

These dependencies only cause distraction when your eyes should be focused on your goals, interests, and passions. Be sure not to compare yourself to people and what they have, either. You'll always find a flaw in your life if you compare yourself to others. And finally, a simple life requires you to enjoy the simpler things in life. Experience every moment as it happens, and stop ruminating on regrets or worrying about tomorrow. Your plans ensure the best results possible, so give this moment everything you have. There's no rush in a simple life.

Step Five: Prioritize

Prioritizing is an essential tool for proper stress management and better living. Imagine yourself in competition against random strangers, or even relatives. The winner is the person who fills their bucket with water first. There's no way for you to win this competition if you're filling everyone else's buckets before paying attention to yours. Another way of looking at priorities is when you have 10 spoons to fill your bucket, and the person next to you is using a cup. They've prioritized their goal, focusing on the most important achievement they wish to accomplish, so they have a huge cup and will win in no time. You, on the other hand, have chosen 10 priorities at once, leaving you with spoons barely capable of filling your neighbor's cup, let alone your bucket.

You have to identify the things that matter the most to you, or you'll be scooping away with menial goals that hardly bring you closer to your outcome. You must reassess your goals, needs, and experiences to be able to focus on what matters. This is the only way you can recognize what needs action right now. Everything further down your to-do list can wait. Determine what your capacity is for new tasks as well, and don't take on what you can't manage. Your priorities should be as clear as daylight, and you must indulge in a little mindful reflection of what you've accomplished at the end of each day. You don't need to pay attention to what you didn't finish because everything has a time and place.

Step Six: Delegate and Eliminate

Would you rather have a suitcase full of what you need, when you need it, and nothing more, or would you prefer to carry a case around that weighs more than you can handle? Sometimes, it's easier said than done to drop tasks we think we need to finish, but prioritizing should've taken care of this burden. An overflowing schedule or weekly planner only leaves your head spinning, making you unable to focus on the tasks that bring you closer to your goals. You have to review your schedule if you find it isn't working anymore. Look for meetings you can cancel or delegate to a colleague, find dinners you can ask the nanny to help you prepare, and cut back on chores that keep you from your goals. Remember that you can automate many of the problems in your schedule, but you need to identify them first. Any task you placed lower on your list of priorities for the week can be eliminated completely, or it can be reassigned to someone else. Perfecting your time management skills allows you to make time for your priorities and avoid the stress accumulation from missing essential tasks.

Step Seven: Communicate Clearly

The lack of effective communication is often the cause of stress when you ask someone to handle a project, let your guard down because you're confident in their abilities, and end up with a mess that you must fix. Clear, concise, and assertive communication should always be a part of your delegations and shared responsibilities. Assertiveness isn't void of politeness in effective communication, so don't be rude or condescending when you tell someone what you would like them to do. Be polite and sincere, and offer clear instructions. Assertive communication can also help us express our concerns, interests, and values so that everyone understands how we feel. Ask for what you need, but explain how you feel about the desired outcome so that there's no miscommunication.

Be firm, empathetic, and fair when you speak, and know exactly what you want. Knowing what you want helps you to be proactive about the outcome. Effective communication is essential at work and home. Don't expect your kids to do their chores if you don't use clear communication, and don't expect your partner to understand how upset you are if they put the potatoes on the stove with the skin on. You told them to peel half the potatoes; you weren't specific enough and should've said to take half the potatoes out of the bag and peel them. In fairness, this is a crazy example, but it could happen if the communication lines aren't effective.

Step Eight: Ask for Help

A nanny or cleaner is a great source of help, but they're automation of your plans. Asking for help when you need it is about realizing that you're struggling to manage your priorities and lead a stress-free life. There's nothing wrong with seeking professional counseling or joining a support group if you have too much on your plate. Support groups are amazing because the people have likely experienced what you're going through now. Friends and relatives don't always understand your struggles, especially if you're recently widowed or divorced. Now, you have the responsibilities you had before with the addition of your partner's duties because they're no longer around. Seeking support before you experience burnout or overwhelming depression and stress is also an option. In fact, it can be part of your strategy from step one. Reach out because you aren't made to handle this life alone when it keeps throwing you with lemons. At some point, you get sick of lemonade.

Step Nine: Learn to Say No

This is a tough step for many people because we have this innate desire to be validated and accepted by the people around us. Think about how many requests you hear in a single day.

"Mom/Dad, I want another cookie!"

"I need you to manage another two clients."

"We need more parents to chaperone the social."

"Can you call this person back to ask her to speak to me again?"

The list is endless. Requests come in many shapes and forms, but at some stage, you need to say no. Saying no might be difficult until you practice it enough, but keep in mind that it frees time to take care of your priorities. A no in one request could lead to a yes in something better. Moreover, you might have time to say yes to something you enjoy. Set healthy boundaries so that you know when to say yes and no. A healthy boundary constitutes what you would allow or not in other people's behaviors.

It also determines how much time and space you need for yourself, which is an essential part of self-care and daily stress management. It also outlines your priorities so that you keep filling your bucket. Having boundaries and saying no isn't a selfish attitude. It shows that you respect your well-being and interests. Be sure to use effective communication to express your boundaries and let your loved ones and colleagues know why you value them. Stop saying yes to activities that bring you no joy, even if you prefer spending the evening at home, sipping hot chocolate, and watching a movie. It's your life, so your boundaries should express that much.

Step Ten: Limit Your Exposure to Stressful People

Some people aren't worth the efforts or emotional drainage. You can't be happy or stress-free if you're surrounded by toxic and fake people who take more than they give. Take an inventory of your interactions and the people you connect with daily. Consider how this person impacts your life. Do they make you laugh? Do they offer support or encourage your dreams? Perhaps, they're the kind of people that drain your energy sources, leaving you feeling worse when you leave their homes. Consider whether each person is a negative or positive influence in your life, and add a tick or cross next to each name. Some friends energize you, pump you with positive thoughts, and make you feel great. Others complain about menial things, always ask for favors, and give nothing in return.

In the middle, you might have friends who offer some support and expect favors from you. The friends who give more than they take can receive a tick, and the friends who take more than they give can receive a cross. These are the friends you must either eliminate or spend limited time with. The middle ground friends who give and take should be weighed on their own scales. If they give more than they take, you can simply limit your exposure to them. However, if they take more than they give, you can eliminate them from your social group. Spend more time with friends who bring you joy, and remember to give back what you receive, but cut loose the fake and pretentious friends. The same applies to relatives, colleagues, and anyone who depletes your positive energy.

Step Eleven: Eliminate Obvious Stressors

Ridding yourself of anything that brings discomfort is instrumental to your well-being. You've already started changing your daily habits, removing caffeine, alcohol, and unhealthy habits, but you need to dig deeper.

Investigate everything you use daily, and determine whether it makes you feel uncomfortable. For example, watching the news has never relieved anyone of stress. It piles stress up until you're buried under it. The news has become so violent because people became desensitized, but that changes. When stress piles up, your sensitivity returns, making you feel the pain of the family looking for their missing child. Social media is another source of countless discomforts. Clean it up so that you have fewer stressors in your digital life.

Remove yourself from groups that don't offer more than they expect from you. Clear your pages, likes, followers, and fake virtual friends so that your social media accounts are conducive to better living. Watch out for the clickbait ads that distract you by promising the world and leaving you with disappointment. Eliminate unnecessary responsibilities you don't benefit from. It doesn't help to have five gym memberships if you joined a yoga class; discontinue some of these to maintain better financial health. Make some changes to your routines, cut hobbies that bore you, and eliminate magazine subscriptions if you don't even read them. The less you have to stress yourself, the more content you'll become.

Planning and organizing can open your life to genuine freedom from stress. These steps change the way it impacts your life, and you can take control of your future. However, what if you were told that you could harness stress to work for you? Before knocking the idea, take a look at the final chapter.

Chapter 8:

Harnessing Stress for Your Benefit

The idea of harnessing stress like a puppet master controlling a puppet seems unfathomable, but the truth is that stress is part of your makeup for a reason. It's there to protect you, and it can be used for improvements in your life if you have control over it. Not every type of stress is bad, and not every situation brings consequences. The good kind of stress can even motivate or inspire you to do great things. Your stress management should remain strong, but there are ways you can turn a negative thing into an opportunity.

Introducing Eustress

If only there was an island where everything we could ever need falls from the sky, and we are left without want or desire. The weather is always perfect, and time doesn't exist in this tropical paradise. We can sleep all we like, take as many walks on the warm beach sand as we want because fatigue doesn't overcome us, and we can explore all day long. How fantastic life would be. Unfortunately, this island doesn't exist, and that's why you need to know that not all stress is bad. Stress is merely a biological response to danger. The stress response or fight or flight mode switches our minds and bodies over to self-preservation when we feel threatened. We either feel the need to fight or flee from the situation. However, stress can also be your best friend when you use it to motivate yourself in a non-life-threatening situation. It's the heightened awareness and focus that helps us knock job interviews and exams out of the park. You've learned about how stress is a perception or belief that you have the supply to feed the demand in any given situation, so it can be a positive experience that prepares you for a challenge when you have the coping mechanisms and management tools to meet the demand.

Everyone uses the word 'stress' as a synonym for distress, but this is a misconception. If you look at the other definitions of the word, stress can also define the elasticity of an object. How elastic is a piece of metal if you apply pressure to it? The composition of the metal determines how much you can manipulate it. Therefore, comparing yourself to a sheet of metal helps you realize that stress is simply the amount of elasticity you have when pressure is applied, and the tools you collected in the previous chapters have altered the amount of pressure required to manipulate your composition. Once you learn how to manage stress constructively, you can challenge yourself to be pressured harder because you have the correct supply for certain types of pressure. Eustress is a word not many people know, but it's a good kind of pressure. It's the kind that challenges you to grow, improve, and master your life. The 'eu' translates directly to 'good,' and this is the kind of stress people use to push themselves to better outcomes. According to Psychologist Kara Fasone, eustress is a different experience altogether (Lindberg & Legg, 2019).

The good kind of stress is the short-lived burst of energy that helps you to complete tasks and solve problematic situations. The natural stress response that ignites your brain to elevate your focus and clarity can increase your performance so that you have more supply to meet the demand. You can focus better on the task, and your quick biological experience doesn't last long enough to cause damage. Eustress is characterized by enhanced concentration, focused energy, motivation, inspiration, and excitement. It's a temporary state where you perceive the threat to be within your capacity. It allows you to challenge yourself to something new and exciting without depleting your resources entirely. Instead, you grow psychologically, emotionally, and physically. Athletes often use this heightened state of focus to improve their performance, bringing them closer to victory.

A runner understands the pressures their body needs to endure so that they can take first place. A swimmer knows that if they challenge their body just a little further, they'll leave their competitors in their wake. Taking on new projects at work also allows successful business people to leverage their existing strengths in a temporary state so that they can consciously push their minds to improve their outcomes. They feel energized enough to master the existing skills and learn new ones. Eustress is also commonly used to expand and set challenging goals that align themselves with your passions and interests. Learning a new skill is already a challenge, and often your goals require this final push. Even traveling is a positive stress experience. Let's face it, traveling is stressful because of all the new environments and uncertain experiences. Arriving in a country where no one speaks English can make you feel lost. You need to find your hotel room, and the language barrier is a problem. However, traveling is a positive experience. It requires short bursts of focused energy to navigate a stream of new things. It's an eye-opener, which teaches you about new cultures and places.

Your knowledge and tolerance of these cultures expands, and the stress you feel is good because it can protect you from a foreign place when you don't know what threats look like. As your experience grows by learning about a foreign country, your guard will ease, and you'll start enjoying new flavors, smells, sights, and sounds. Another way eustress is used daily is through physical conditioning. Your muscles won't grow stronger if you don't challenge them with exercise, which also improves your stamina and strength. Weightlifting provides the pressure muscles need to enhance themselves, and that's what makes eustress an invaluable tool for physical endurance. The desire to avoid stress is natural, but without the good kind of stress, you can't grow, expand, and become your best self. Positive stress leads to positive changes in your life, so consider how you can use the experience to learn and adapt when you feel pressured. The secret with eustress is that you should always keep the characteristics in mind.

Ask yourself whether you've wanted to be average at life, or do you want to master it? Maybe you want to master a talent or your career, but the fear of succumbing to stress is enough to freeze you. You can't hide from stress if you want to be the best version of yourself. Managing stress is one thing, but mastering your responses means that you need to turn discomfort into opportunity. To be fulfilled or actualized in life, one needs to feel like you're in control of it. You can't be truly happy unless you have control over every controllable aspect of life. Changing your perception of stress is easier once you know how to manage it. The truth is that too little stress leads to a boring life, poor attention, missed opportunities, and confusion. Too much of it can lead to burnout, poor health, and unwanted outcomes. However, in the center is eustress, which helps you find emotional balance, focused attention, and rational thinking.

Psychologist Mihaly Csikszentmihalyi explains that the true key to happiness and a life worth living is to reach the flow state, which is also achieved through experiencing eustress (Tocino-Smith, 2019). The flow state is when you become engulfed and lost in your experience, such as playing a musical instrument. A challenge exists, but you're prepared to push yourself to meet the demand. You know that it's possible to achieve your desired outcome, but you also have a deep passion for growth. You know exactly what you need to do, but you enter the flow state, allowing eustress to move you to mastery. Imagine turning your life into a flow state. It's as close as you'll ever come to the island because you're in full control of your beliefs, perceptions, responses, and outcomes.

How to Master Stress

Reaching the thrilling high that comes with positive stress means that you need to include it in your life. You should learn something new every day, whether it's a small fact or a life-changing skill. Step out of the workplace comfort zone, and this might require the adoption of a new skill or responsibility. Exercise routines are the simplest form of using eustress to your advantage. If you're jogging for 20 minutes this week, push it to 25 minutes next week. Increase your weights as your stamina and endurance grow. Moreover, learn to start setting goals that challenge you enough to encourage your growth. They should be realistic so that distress doesn't overwhelm the motivation and focus you seek. You want challenging goals in your personal and professional life. An essential part of goal-setting is that you track your progress. This holds you accountable, and it gives you inspiration for improvements and new opportunities. Learn how to make stress your advantage, and your perception of your life will change while you make the most of it.

Leverage Stress

Take a moment to consider your capacity for potential because chances are that it's far greater than you think. Use the leverage you have with eustress to condition better outcomes from your goals and desires. You can use stressful deadlines to improve your chances of success because external factors, such as finishing a project on time so that you can earn a promotion motivates you to get your work done. Hold yourself accountable to a deadline that impacts the people in your life, whether it's at work or home. Don't allow your deadlines to cause paralyzing doubt. Make sure you have the necessary skills and coping mechanisms to handle a project before leveraging stress. A deadline is a promise made to yourself and the people involved, especially if your boss expects a presentation on Monday. It's also a promise you make to your kids when you challenge yourself to finish building the treehouse over the weekend. Recognize whether your capacity can meet the potential outcome, but remember to keep your excitement at the frontline with a little complexity. Don't attempt to master eustress if you're setting unrealistic deadlines and making promises that can't be met.

Develop Resilience Through Positive Experiences

One fact we love denying is that the more we fail, the more we learn and grow. Resilience is a flawed concept if you aren't exposed to the experience of stressful situations. The only way you can build an unshakable emotional resilience is to expose yourself to controlled stressors according to the American Institute of Stress (Heckman, 2019). Hiding under a rock won't help you learn how to cope with situations, and your resilience can decline when life chooses to challenge you. Eustress allows you to put yourself in situations where you're in control of stress so that you can develop the skills to combat it, which might be mindfulness or lifestyle changes. To make the experience positive, you must step out of your comfort zone and into a safe environment that doesn't cause distress but rather a challenge. When things go south, you'll have what you need to deal with negative stress because you know what helped you through a previous challenge.

You'll develop the ability to operate rationally when the cards fall. For example, challenge yourself by signing up for a course to enhance your career. Indeed, your schedule and planning will change, but this alone provides a challenge. You'll need to make time for studies and class, and your current life doesn't pause while you're busy. Another example would be to learn a new skill to develop your talents. Maybe you've always been passionate about painting, but your ability to paint faces isn't something to brag about. You have some level of skills and experience, but you need guidance to improve your talent. There's a fine line between a positive and negative challenge. Don't take on a new responsibility at work if you don't have the skills or experience. Rather study until you have the minimal requirements, and then you can challenge yourself to new opportunities at work. Use realistic goals to improve your resilience, but don't overdo it so that you become distressed. Small steps are better than leaping into a shark tank.

Look for Blind Spots

Sometimes, a distressing situation is shaded by blind spots, and if you identify them, you won't find the situation distressing anymore. Stress should be viewed as an opportunity to learn more about the triggers that cause it. Not all stressors need to remain uncomfortable. Let's say that a mother feels like her parenting skills aren't working for her teenage son. He's all over the place, ignoring her, disrespecting her, and doing what he wants, which sounds like the typical teenager, right? The mother deems parenting a stressful experience, and she might be afraid of having another child. The mistake she made is that she generalized one situation as a cart of bad apples. She didn't look deeper into the reasons why parenting makes her miserable.

She needs to ask herself what it is about the situation that makes her feel overwhelmed. The answer lies within her question, and it uncovers triggers to make the same situation more tolerable in the future. Perhaps, her son's lack of communication and ignorance is what grinds her. Until she investigates the reasons why she feels like a failed parent, she won't understand why her friends call parenting a unique kind of heaven. She identifies the main reasons for her concerns, and she buys a few books on how to communicate with and discipline a teenage boy. Voila, her most distressing moments become history. Looking for blind spots means that you need to identify learning opportunities in a stressful situation so that it becomes less distressing.

Adopt Self-Awareness

Denying the fact that stress is unavoidable is like chopping your own fingers off. Life will always evolve into new challenges, expectations, and opportunities. You can't walk with your head down, pretending that stress doesn't impact you. It exists, and it will continue to test you when you least expect it, so don't feel the need to live in a life of peace alone. Stress is an ongoing factor of life, so your attitude, lifestyle, philosophy, and management should be persistent. What also needs to remain in your awareness is that your perception of stress will ebb and flow as life takes you down different paths in your career and at home. Believing that your career remains static will only set you up for distress when something goes wrong. Expect challenges to rise, and prepare yourself to face them. The day you stop expecting stress to vanish is the day you'll learn to work with it, and you'll be able to use it to grow and be your best self. Eustress must become something you look forward to so that you can always find the key to executing effective management and know when you need to pull extra weight.

Welcome Creativity

Life is unpredictable, and so is every situation that causes stress. Everyone loves familiarity because it brings comfort, but imagine how boring life would be if you removed uncertainty, mystery, and unforeseen circumstances. Excitement is part of eustress, and you can't master your stress if you don't get creative. Stop allowing stress to deter you from potential inspiration and creativity. Rather look at it as though it brings answers to questions you might not have asked yet. Don't concern yourself incessantly about making a living. Use your worries to design a life worth living, one in which you're successful, happy, and have a purpose. You can't be the mogul of your industry if you aren't creative though. Using your stress creatively allows you to turn unpredictable questions into answers that wow people.

Use the adrenaline pumping through your veins to create the possibility of innovation, excitement, and risk-taking that might lead to great triumph. Take control of positive stress, and challenge yourself to find an answer that wasn't seen before. Let's say that you're an architect who must design new twin buildings. The skyscrapers are on opposite sides of the road, and the company motto is "transparency is key." Suddenly, you put the motto into your design with a subtle change by making the interconnecting bridge restaurant fully transparent. The client loves your design because it's creative to have his buildings promote the company motto without words. Use stress to be creative, and watch your life turn into something unpredictably good.

Enhance Your Priorities

In the last chapter, you set your priorities straight, but now you can enhance the main goals and ambitions you have in life by adding eustress to the mix. Take on a new challenge to pursue your main priority, and don't forget to set a deadline to turn it into a positively stressful goal. Your focused attention during the stress response can increase the chances of succeeding, so make it count. Your priority can't be to live a stress-free life because this doesn't help you grow. So, redefine your definition of freedom from stress. Your freedom should be in the form of control. Know that you can't avoid stress altogether, so prioritize the situations and goals that push you forward in life. You might have to review your priorities once more.

Adding priorities that challenge you can help you regain control over your workload in your career. It can help you maintain consistency at home. If you planned your stressful situations at later times during your day, change them. Bring the stressful work and home responsibilities to your mornings so that you can energize your focus to accomplish tasks early in the day. Make calls to clients as soon as you get into the office, and prepare dinner before leaving for work. This way, your lower priorities or less stressful situations are left for later in the day, making you more capable of having the energy left to deal with unexpected stressors if they come. You have more mental energy in the morning, so dedicate yourself to using eustress for growth when your mind is at its peak.

Increase Opportunity

Any stress indicates that a challenge lies ahead, and sometimes, this challenge hides an opportunity. Using your controlled stress, you can effectively identify the opportunities before they slip by. It doesn't matter if the opportunity shows you the need to change direction, increase your knowledge, rise up, or try something new. It might be showing you how to move around perceived failure because what some people see as failures, others see as new doorways to greater possibilities. Eustress is proven to enhance your intelligence and cognitive abilities, so find ways you can learn new skills and develop a level of knowledge that promotes your life (Campbell, 2017).

Even if you don't want to stay in your current career or you aren't concerned about a promotion, take a class to learn something you've never known. Not everything you learn and improve needs to align itself with your current life and career projections. Maybe you're a marketing guru, but you've always been fascinated by the human mind. These two things don't seem related, but they can be. Understanding the works of the human mind can help you improve your current marketing strategies, or you can redirect your career to become a counselor or life coach. Don't cut your wings by restricting yourself to one field. Explore new horizons, and allow opportunities to become realities.

Welcome Stress and Strategize

Success shouldn't be something you win or inherit. The only way it can become your source of happiness and fulfillment is if you welcome the journey it brings, including the challenges, mistakes, and new directions. It's the only way you can evolve your talents, skills, or self. Expect there to be a struggle, and welcome it with open arms. Working under pressure and being frustrated only makes the accomplishment more enjoyable. Enjoy the journey because the struggles bring potential for true actualization. The more you overcome, the more you realize that your design, by nature, is to thrive. Welcome inspiration rather than focusing on desperation. Nothing has ever been worthwhile unless you struggled to get it. Otherwise, you wouldn't appreciate it as much as you do after the long battle.

Develop a strategy where stress can move you through achievements and accomplishments you never thought possible. Surprise yourself because people tend to want the relief after pressure more than anything else. What the relief brings is entirely up to you. Don't be impulsive though because this could leave you with a mess that takes a lot of energy to clean. Go back to your planning in the previous chapter, and design a strategy that offers enough positive stress without guaranteed implosions. Slow down, and think about your goals so that you ensure a balance between peace and eustress. You also don't want to be on a constant high, and you certainly don't want impulsivity to rule your chance of success. Keep in mind that eustress awakens your rational thoughts, so if you find yourself strategizing unrealistically, you might not be experiencing positive stress.

Collaborate

One fact that doesn't change between eustress and distress is that a network of the right people can aid your journey. It's not so much about needing support from them in positive situations, but rather about collaborating with like-minded, positive, and motivated individuals to move past an obstacle you might be facing. Stress automatically forces you to reach out when it becomes overwhelming, but you can use this to your advantage. Gathering advice, recommendations, and new ideas from your team at work or your support network at home can help you see previously missed opportunities. Successful people brainstorm and collaborate with others. This also guarantees that they never feel like they must have all the answers because eustress becomes distress when the weight becomes unbearable.

Look for Signals

By now, you know how it feels when you become overwhelmed. You know how your muscles tense up, and you feel your heart racing in the face of a task that requires completion. The final tool to use stress to your advantage is to know your signals. Know when your brain is activating the stress response, and learn to recognize whether it's a simple discomfort or you're feeling horrified. Whatever the signal tells you, remind yourself to remain positive. Optimism is the key to using stress for your benefit because your perceptions and evaluation of the situation determine the outcome of your response. Learn to recognize the changes in your body quickly so that you can remind yourself of the potential for an opportunity if the situation doesn't pose a real threat. Activate positive beliefs, which is possible now that you know about eustress, and use these beliefs to diligently focus on the possible solutions to a problem before freaking out.

The best kind of stress management isn't to live a stress-free life. Indeed, it's what we aim for most of the day, but you need to add stressful motivations to grow if you want more than a peaceful life. A peaceful life doesn't guarantee a happy life, but being in full control of your response to stress is as close as you can come to happiness and success.

Conclusion

Stress has been like an iron fist in your life. It's plagued many parts of your life, from work to home, and from children to friends, and its sole intention was to strip you of happiness, health, and the best version of yourself. There's no need for the hold it has over you anymore. You don't need to worry about your daily responsibilities weighing on you, dragging you to your low-point when you try to handle everything. Everyone desires a balance between their obligations and their sanity, but the gap grows larger and larger without proper stress management.

No one deserves to feel the pressure building under the surface until it explodes, especially not you. You've known that this isn't the way you should feel. Between the children screaming, your employer demanding the world of you, and your friends claiming that you have no time for them anymore, you've succumbed to the pressures of life. Being an entrepreneur isn't any easier. Establishing your own business is something that requires hard work and sleepless nights, but it should lead to a feeling of accomplishment at some point. The harder the struggle, the more successful you're supposed to be, right?

The sleepless nights can't continue if you desire the best outcome. Feeling like a drained zombie, dragging your feet from one step to another, isn't the healthiest way to live. Stress has an unkind face, tugging at your health and mental well-being as you continue the uphill battle. How can some people claim to use stress as leverage? How can they be so successful when life laughs in their face? Moreover, they tend to enjoy their families, always having time to do what they want with their kids. Instead, parenting has become another chore, one that doesn't look like the movies.

Parenting is supposed to be the highlight of your life, but it's been everything else. It's those lost nights of sleep, the slow grind of work, and the struggle with daily obligations among a myriad of other things that makes parenting less of a joy. It's no surprise that you think you'll go crazy under the weight of this burdensome curse. It certainly doesn't help when you feel depressed and anxious, either. The more you believe that life is wrong and that you should be enjoying the little moments, the more life kicks you down, taking your happiness along with it. This isn't a fair way to live.

Fairness is a life filled with smiles and laughter. It's a life void of confusion and brain fog that often comes with uncontrolled and mismanaged stress. Fairness is being able to relax and let go of the worries that plague your mind. It's the ability to maintain optimal health and use coping mechanisms to deal with the crutch that is the stress curse. Fairness is your idea of handling stressful situations without them overwhelming you. However, you can't deny the truth anymore. Fairness is only achievable if you take back control of your life. Your life can't change unless you grab hold of the reins.

Fortunately, you know how to regain control now. You've learned about the true meaning of a life worth living and how you can sustain it long-term. You know how stress is beating you like a drum, mentally, physically, and emotionally to change you into someone you don't wish to be. You've learned about how stress interferes with your career, whether you're employed by someone or you're striving to build your own empire. You also know how stress has disrupted your meaningful relationships, tearing them apart. There's no need for this debilitating thorn that steals every good part of your life.

Recognizing where stress comes from, and the many masks it can wear, has helped you understand why you need to change your life. You can't fall into the habits that bring long-term challenges. Taking back control became simpler once you recognized your triggers and the detrimental coping strategies you thought were helping, even the stress outlets you weren't aware of. You've replaced these unhealthy strategies with genuine tactics, some of which only take up to a minute. Emergency strategies aside, you also know how to change your mindset and adopt a new response to stress.

Stress was once rightfully feared because you didn't understand it, but now, you look for an opportunity in the midst of the burden. You've also adopted a new lifestyle, which helps you list the fog away from your future. Sometimes, it's as easy as learning how to breathe properly, and other times, you can implement mindfulness techniques that reduce the weight of this curse. Stress doesn't seem like a heavy burden once you know how to activate the relaxation response, which is a neurological guarantee. Taking back control has nothing to do with fairy tale endings and unrealistic ideations.

Your ability to control the mountain in front of you lies within science and biology, but the practices are enjoyable and simple enough for anyone to learn. Your entire lifestyle can change to ensure better outcomes. You can direct your future to find your best self, health, success, and happiness. Moreover, it isn't complicated to manage stress while taking care of yourself. In fact, omitting the self-care part of this journey will destroy the foundation of a better life. Adopt the steps required to plan and control your life so that stress can't grab hold of you again.

Preparing for the war against this curse increases your chances of success against the enemy. Within all the knowledge you've gathered lies a secret. Not every stressful situation heads a warning. Some situations can be used to progress your life and career. Becoming the master of your stress with simple techniques, different responses, and a new perspective is the way you manage the curse so that it has no impact on your life or health. You have mental exercises, stress management techniques, and mindfulness in the hat of many options on your side.

It's time to make a decision now that every stress management tool is under your belt. Do you want to live under the extraordinary weight of stress, or do you want to become the master of everything to come? If you choose to be the master, go out there and apply the stress management knowledge you've gained to take back control of your life.

References

ADAA. (2000). *Exercise for stress and anxiety.* Anxiety and Depression Association of America. https://adaa.org/living-with-anxiety/managing-anxiety/exercise-stress-and-anxiety

Al Sunni, A., & Latif, R. (2014). Effects of chocolate intake on perceived stress; a controlled clinical study. *International Journal of Health Sciences, 8*(4), 393–401. https://www.ncbi.nlm.nih.gov/pmc/articles/PMC4350893/

Alidina, S. (2018, August 15). *9 ways mindfulness reduces stress.* Mindful. https://www.mindful.org/9-ways-mindfulness-reduces-stress/

Awake and Mindful. (2018, April 23). *Free guided meditations to relieve stress.* Awake & Mindful. https://awakeandmindful.com/free-guided-meditations-to-relieve-stress/

Babauta, L. (n.d.). *27 great tips to keep your life organized.* Zen Habits. https://zenhabits.net/27-great-tips-to-keep-your-life-organized/

Batson, J. (2011). *Stress research*. The American Institute of Stress. https://www.stress.org/stress-research

Becker, J. (2019, October 22). *10 creative ways to declutter your home*. Becoming a Minimalist. https://www.becomingminimalist.com/creative-ways-to-declutter/

Bethune, S. (2007). *Stress A major health problem in the U.S., warns APA*. APA PsycNet. https://www.apa.org/news/press/releases/2007/10/stress

Boston University. (n.d.). *Build resilience and cope with stress*. Boston University School of Public Health. https://sphweb.bumc.bu.edu/otlt/MPH-Modules/PH/Stress-Resilience/Stress-Resilience_print.html

Boyd, D. (2019, September 23). *42 worrying workplace stress statistics*. The American Institute of Stress. https://www.stress.org/42-worrying-workplace-stress-statistics

Brown, A. (2019, July 4). *62 stress management techniques, strategies & activities*. Positive Psychology. https://positivepsychology.com/stress-management-techniques-tips-burn-out/

Buckley, C. (2014, June 20). *How to respond to stress before it gets worse*. Coaching Positive Performance.

https://www.coachingpositiveperformance.com/respond-to-stress/

Business. (2020, April 1). *How stress connects to productivity.* Business. https://www.business.com/articles/stress-and-productivity-what-the-numbers-say/

Campbell, S. (2017, November 9). *10 ways to use stress to your advantage.* Entrepreneur. https://www.entrepreneur.com/article/304288

Clark, M. (2018, April 5). *How decluttering your space could make you healthier and happier.* Mayo Clinic. https://www.mayoclinic.org/healthy-lifestyle/stress-management/in-depth/how-decluttering-your-space-could-make-you-healthier-and-happier/art-20390064

Czernik, A. B. (2015, June 19). *Managing stress and building resilience.* Coaching & Consulting - Inspired Executives. https://www.inspired-executives.com/managing-stress-building-resilience-quick-tips/

Delegran, L., & Evans, R. (2014). *Mindfulness for stress reduction.* University of Minnesota - Taking Charge of Your Health and Well-Being. https://www.takingcharge.csh.umn.edu/mindfulness-stress-reduction

Domes, Z. (2013, May 14). *How to organize your life: 10 habits of really organized people.* Lifehack;

https://www.lifehack.org/articles/productivity/how-organize-your-life-10-habits-really-organized-people.html

Edney, L. (2012, December 5). *5 steps to find peace instead of stressing about the future.* Tiny Buddha. https://tinybuddha.com/blog/5-steps-to-find-peace-instead-of-stressing-about-the-future/

Eisler, M. (2017, August 11). *How to react to stress in a healthy way.* Melissa Eisler. https://melissaeisler.com/react-stress-healthy-way/

Engel, B. (2018, June 19). *Using the practice of self-kindness to cope with stress.* Psychology Today. https://www.psychologytoday.com/us/blog/the-compassion-chronicles/201806/using-the-practice-self-kindness-cope-stress

Felman, A. (2020, March 12). *Stress: Why does it happen and how can we manage it?* Medical News Today. https://www.medicalnewstoday.com/articles/145855#causes

Fowler, P. (2018, January 11). *Breathing techniques for stress relief.* WebMD; https://www.webmd.com/balance/stress-management/stress-relief-breathing-techniques#1

Gilles, G. (n.d.). *Build up your resilience to stressful life events - dealing with stress and anxiety management coping mechanisms*. Mental Help. https://www.mentalhelp.net/blogs/build-up-your-resilience-to-stressful-life-events/

Goodful. (2020). *10-Minute meditation for stress*. YouTube. https://www.youtube.com/watch?v=z6X5oEIg6Ak

Halkos, G., & Bousinakis, D. (2010). The effect of stress and satisfaction on productivity. *International Journal of Productivity and Performance Management, 59*(5), 415–431. https://doi.org/10.1108/17410401011052869

Hamilton, A., & Gallo, L. (2015, March). *Speaking of psychology: The stress of money*. APA. https://www.apa.org/research/action/speaking-of-psychology/financial-stress

Heart. (2014). *3 tips to manage stress*. Heart.org. https://www.heart.org/en/healthy-living/healthy-lifestyle/stress-management/3-tips-to-manage-stress

Heckman, W. (2019, October 21). *The good stress: How eustress helps you grow*. The American Institute of Stress. https://www.stress.org/the-good-stress-how-eustress-helps-you-grow

Hill, C. (2018, December 17). *This is the no. 1 reason Americans are so stressed out*. Market Watch. https://www.marketwatch.com/story/one-big-reason-americans-are-so-stressed-and-unhealthy-2018-10-11

Hitti, M. (2009, June 19). *Causes of stress.* WebMD; https://www.webmd.com/balance/guide/causes-of-stress#1

Jana, R. (2020, July 8). *How to make stress work to your advantage.* Inc.com. https://www.inc.com/raj-jana/how-to-make-stress-work-to-your-advantage.html

Jenkins, R. (2018, January 8). *Know your stress triggers.* CABA. https://www.caba.org.uk/help-and-guides/information/know-your-stress-triggers

Johannson, A. (2019, March 25). *3 ways to respond to stressful situations more calmly.* Thrive Global. https://thriveglobal.com/stories/3-ways-to-respond-to-stressful-situations-more-calmly/

Kivi, R. (2012, September 28). *Acute stress disorder.* Healthline; https://www.healthline.com/health/acute-stress-disorder

Lauretta, A. (2020, November 2). *5 (actually healthy) ways to deal with stress.* Women's Running. https://www.womensrunning.com/health/wellness/5-healthy-stressful-situations/

Levine, H. (n.d.). *Can stress affect your ability to conceive?* WebMD.

https://www.webmd.com/baby/features/infertility-stress#1

Liddon, A. (2009, May 22). *Our goals: Eustress and distress.* Oh She Glows. https://ohsheglows.com/2009/05/22/our-goals-eustress-and-distress/

Lindberg, S., & Legg, T. J. (2019, January 3). *Eustress: The good stress.* Healthline. https://www.healthline.com/health/eustress

Liquido, K. (2014, October 23). *Get better at handling stress by fighting these 10 unhealthy habits.* Verily. https://verilymag.com/2014/10/unhealthy-habits-how-to-handle-stress

Lisa. (2019, May 31). *How to detach yourself from your thoughts using mindfulness.* Pinnable Beauty. https://pinnablebeauty.com/how-to-detach-yourself-from-your-thoughts/

Lowin, R. (2015, May 15). *How cleaning up helped one woman lose 50 pounds.* Today. https://www.today.com/home/study-shows-cleaning-your-home-can-help-you-lose-weight-t22131

Mayo Clinic Staff. (2018, July 6). *Post-traumatic stress disorder (PTSD) - symptoms and causes.* Mayo Clinic. https://www.mayoclinic.org/diseases-conditions/post-traumatic-stress-disorder/symptoms-causes/syc-20355967

Mayo Clinic Staff. (2019a). *Identify your stress triggers.* Mayo Clinic. https://www.mayoclinic.org/healthy-lifestyle/stress-management/in-depth/stress-management/art-20044151

Mayo Clinic Staff. (2019b, April 12). *Stress management: Examine your stress reaction.* Mayo Clinic. https://www.mayoclinic.org/healthy-lifestyle/stress-management/in-depth/stress-management/art-20044289

Meadowglade. (2019, July 19). *What an unhealthy coping mechanism looks like.* The Meadowglade. https://themeadowglade.com/what-an-unhealthy-coping-mechanism-looks-like/

Mellor, S. (2013). *Use mindfulness to manage stress.* Skills You Need. https://www.skillsyouneed.com/rhubarb/manage-stress-with-mindfulness.html

Mellowed. (2019, March 8). *10 unhealthy ways to cope with stress.* Mellowed. https://mellowed.com/unhealthy-ways-to-cope-with-stress/

Mental Help. (n.d.). *Stress management techniques.* Mental Help. https://www.mentalhelp.net/stress/management-techniques/

Mills, H., Reiss, N., & Dombeck, M. (n.d.). *Types of stressors (eustress vs. distress) - stress reduction and management.* Helen Farabee. https://www.helenfarabee.org/poc/view_doc.php?type=doc&id=15644&cn=117

Mineo, L. (2018, April 17). *Less stress, clearer thoughts with mindfulness meditation.* Harvard Gazette. https://news.harvard.edu/gazette/story/2018/04/less-stress-clearer-thoughts-with-mindfulness-meditation/

Morin, A. (2017, May 13). *6 ways to stop stressing about things you can't control.* Forbes. https://www.forbes.com/sites/amymorin/2017/05/13/6-ways-to-stop-stressing-about-things-you-cant-control/?sh=18fc0e5030db

National Institute of Mental Health. (n.d.). *5 things you should know about stress.* National Institute of Mental Health. https://www.nimh.nih.gov/health/publications/stress/index.shtml

National Institutes of Health. (n.d.). *7 steps to manage stress and build resilience.* National Institutes of Health. https://orwh.od.nih.gov/in-the-spotlight/all-articles/7-steps-manage-stress-and-build-resilience

Neuro Care. (n.d.). *Understanding stress disorders.* Neuro Care.

https://neurocareclinics.com.au/understanding-stress-disorders/

Olivo, E. (2015, January 2). *Why acceptance is one of the best stress reducers.* Psychology Today. https://www.psychologytoday.com/us/blog/wise-mind-living/201501/why-acceptance-is-one-the-best-stress-reducers

Pagan, C. N. (2018, January 11). *What is aromatherapy?* WebMD; https://www.webmd.com/balance/stress-management/aromatherapy-overview#1

Patterson, E. (2019, May 6). *Stress statistics.* The Recovery Village. https://www.therecoveryvillage.com/mental-health/stress/related/stress-statistics/

Resnick, N. (2018, July 18). *5 scientific reasons decluttering your home will make you happier.* Thrive Global. https://thriveglobal.com/stories/5-scientific-reasons-decluttering-your-home-will-make-you-happier/

Rieglar, T. (2019, June 25). *5 simple living habits that actually reduce stress and anxiety.* Tertia Riegler. https://www.tertiariegler.com/reduce-stress-simplify-life/

Robbins, T. (2015, July 14). *The negative effects of stress on a relationship.* Tony Robbins.

https://www.tonyrobbins.com/health-vitality/what-is-the-impact-of-your-stress/

Scott, E. (2006, January 23). *17 highly effective stress relievers.* Verywell Mind; https://www.verywellmind.com/tips-to-reduce-stress-3145195

Scott, E. (2019). *9 ways to be more resilient in the face of stress.* Verywell Mind. https://www.verywellmind.com/cope-with-stress-and-become-more-resilient-3144889

Scott, E. (2020, September 17). *Why avoidance coping creates additional stress.* Verywell Mind. https://www.verywellmind.com/avoidance-coping-and-stress-4137836#:~:text=Avoidance%20coping%20involves%20trying%20to

Shifts. (2019, April 18). *9 unhealthy ways of coping with stress.* Shifts Coaching. https://shifts.coach/stress-management/unhealthy-ways-deal-stress/

Silverman, A. (2012). *How to reduce stress through mindfulness.* University of Washington. http://agerrtc.washington.edu/info/factsheets/mindfulness

Sorgen, C. (n.d.). *Cut the stress from your life.* WebMD. https://www.webmd.com/a-to-z-guides/features/cut-stress-simplify-life#1

Stibich, M. (2020, February 4). *Managing the stressful people in your life for better health.* Verywell Mind. https://www.verywellmind.com/how-to-manage-stressful-people-2223890

Stoppler, M. C., & Dryden-Edwards, R. (2019). *Stress symptoms and stress management.* MedicineNet. https://www.medicinenet.com/stress/article.htm

Suttie, J. (2019, October 28). *The mindfulness skill that is crucial for stress.* Greater Good. https://greatergood.berkeley.edu/article/item/the_mindfulness_skill_that_is_crucial_for_stress

Swedish Blogger. (2017, May 16). *How decluttering can improve physical and mental health.* Swedish Blog. https://blog.swedish.org/swedish-blog/how-decluttering-can-improve-physical-and-mental-health

Tocino-Smith, J. (2019, July 4). *What is eustress and how is it different than stress?* Positive Psychology. https://positivepsychology.com/what-is-eustress/

WebMD. (n.d.). *Stress management.* WebMD. https://www.webmd.com/balance/stress-management/stress-management#3

WebMD. (2017). *The effects of stress on your body.* WebMD; https://www.webmd.com/balance/stress-management/effects-of-stress-on-your-body

www.ingramcontent.com/pod-product-compliance
Lightning Source LLC
Chambersburg PA
CBHW050320120526
44592CB00014B/1980